ADVANCE PRAISE FOR MOM.B.A.

"If every young professional reads this book our future will be in great hands. It is an amazing compilation of life's most critical lessons. Bravo to Schoenbart's success as a mother and leader."

– Lynnette Cooke, global CEO, Kantar Health

"This is the comprehensive guide that will certainly prepare those seeking excellence in areas of business and personal success. From the personal stories and lessons of leadership, interpersonal skills, networking, sales strategy, and so much more, this book should be on the list for everyone who is on the journey of improvement in their professional and personal worlds."

– Robert Fishman, partner, Sandler Training

"Whether you are just starting your career or someone like myself who has been in business for over 30 years, there are insightful pointers in this book that can truly help everyone."

– Ivy Solowiejczyk, vice president, IBM

"Of the many business books that are published every year, rarely are they this wide-ranging and practical. A world of applicable lessons for both the young and the experienced professional."

– Rich Isaac, president, Sandler Training

"Listen to your MOM! A practical guide to applying human logic to business and increasing your odds at succeeding and doing what you love."

– Ali Charri
senior vice president, Strategy and Insights, Darden Restaurants

"Mom.B.A. is casual and warm, yet full of wisdom and influence. It achieves the perfect balance in mixing personal stories with real business experience that supports the key points."

– Stephanie Dismore
vice president and general manager, HP

"Schoenbart's book fulfills a real and meaningful need. Her unique voice comes through, and her perspective is valuable to new college graduates and beyond."

– Lynda Firey-Oldroyd
senior director of consumer research, Starbucks

Ever Wish Your Mother Was a CEO?

Mom.B.A.

Essential Business Advice from One Generation to the Next

By Karyn Schoenbart

with Alexandra Levit

Published by Motivational Press, Inc.
1777 Aurora Road
Melbourne, Florida, 32935
www.MotivationalPress.com

Manufactured in the United States of America.

ISBN: 978-1-62865-458-5

CONTENTS

To my daughter, Danielle
The inspiration for this book

And to the men in my life
My loving husband, Brad
My caring son, Eric
and my always supportive business partner, Tod

FOREWORD

DANIELLE SPORKIN

A YEAR AFTER I GRADUATED from college and was settling into the working world—such as accepting that spring break and summer vacation no longer existed—a funny thing happened: my friends started calling me for career advice. Whenever they had questions about work, from dealing with a difficult boss to how to ask for a promotion, they sought me out and asked my opinion. And it was more than needing someone to vent to or bounce around ideas with: they saw me as an authority on professional development matters. But why? It's not as though I had been working longer or had more experience.

And then it hit me. Of course! I had over 30 years of business experience behind me. Or in other words, I had my mother.

I can't remember a time when Mom didn't work. She's a lifelong career woman. Sure, there were periods in my life when I resented her for it, like when other kids' moms attended field trips or picked them up after school. But as I grew older and began to understand all the skills I'd learned from her and their application in my own professional life, it made up for the missed soccer practices in spades.

I first felt Mom's influence when I was fairly young. In preschool, when all the other kids said they wanted to be ballerinas or princesses when they grew up, I wanted to be a vice president. Of what, I didn't know. But my mom was one, so I was determined to be one too.

Mom and I didn't play house or store, we played "the interview game," and by 11-years- old, I had honed my skills. I didn't have a resume or any work experience, but I could calmly and rationally answer questions about my strengths, weaknesses, and "if I were an animal, what I would be?" better than some recent college graduates.

In middle school, I built book reports in PowerPoint with full slide animation. And by high school, I had mastered the art of the pitch because every sleepover party during my childhood required a business plan presentation. By the time I entered the corporate world, I was ready.

Being raised by a strong female business leader who passed on important lessons through her own experiences armed me with useful and transferable skills. For example, when I'd get in trouble as a kid, I learned "Sorry, but..." doesn't work because the "but" essentially negates the apology. No one likes to be wrong or admit they messed up, but knowing how to properly apologize and own up to your mistakes is an important trait.

I also learned from Mom how to navigate sticky social situations. In school, I was bullied and sometimes had trouble fitting in. So, when I got my first job and experienced cliques in the workplace, Mom told me "work is not high school." Once again, she was right.

Today, I'm a successful business woman in my own right, and I'm not only applying what I've learned from my mother but also gaining my own experiences, and sometimes teaching Mom a thing or two! I've also realized it's not all roses when it comes to having a mother mentor. Sometimes, I'll call after a bad day at work looking for a little nurturing, and instead I'll get a speech about how I could have handled the situation better or what I could do differently in the future. While I appreciate Mom's advice, there are times when I just want her to tell me everything will be all right. But overall, I wouldn't have it any other way.

I encouraged my mother to share her stories and lessons so that others could benefit from her experiences as I have, and that's how Mom.B.A was conceived. Regardless of whether you are just starting out, whether you are ready for the next level, or even whether you are the parent of a young professional, you can learn from my mother's perspectives on leadership, professional growth, and work/life integration. Mom and I have had so many talks about these topics at our kitchen table and in the car, and I'm glad to lend her to you. By the time you finish reading Mom.B.A, you won't need a CEO for a mom. You'll have the business wisdom of 30 years to call on—guidance I'm sure will serve you well now and in the years to come.

Danielle Sporkin

INTRODUCTION

When asked how I rose to my position and what someone should do to achieve similar success, I've said: "work hard and get promoted." If pushed, I might add "volunteer for things," but that was generally the extent of it. Neither of my parents went to college, and I wanted to be a second-grade teacher when I grew up. I didn't know anything about a career in business, and I fell into my first job in market research. I didn't have a grand plan, and I never imagined myself being chief executive officer of a multi-million dollar global company!

When my daughter Danielle graduated from college and started working, I discovered she had picked up scores of business tips from me that I had learned over the course of my career. To my surprise, I had been teaching them to her throughout her childhood without even realizing it.

While I didn't have formal business training, through over 30+ years of work experience I had amassed lessons that could, well, fill a book.

When Danielle discovered others could benefit from my experiences, she suggested I write this book, and the title was her idea. My husband was supportive, as well, and when I said I was concerned I didn't have a business degree, he shared his perspective. As a doctor, he had many years of formal education. He told me about conventional wisdom in medicine: all you learn in medical school is the terminology. You learn how to be a doctor in your first year of internship. Then, the rest of your career is spent honing those skills.

I decided to take on the challenge of authoring this book, and once I started writing, I couldn't stop. I've really enjoyed sharing my personal anecdotes about how I gained a variety of skills over years of increasing responsibility. Most of the concepts in this book are not rocket science. They are practical, easy to grasp tips that work in today's business environment. I hope my experiences as a mother and a CEO can propel you to succeed in your career—perhaps faster and further than you thought possible.

Here's our roadmap. In the first chapter, you'll learn how to master the first impression, including dressing appropriately and making lasting, human connections. In the second, we'll move on to different aspects of networking, such as building effective professional relationships and coping with the social politics of the workplace. We'll delve more deeply into managerial relationships, such as getting along with your supervisors in the third chapter and managing others in the fourth.

Chapter five will focus on dealing with workplace conflict, including difficult colleagues and clients, and chapters six through ten are what we refer to as the "empowerment chapters." Here, we'll discuss how to put forth the best you and develop essential business skills, how to increase your global footprint and be an effective leader, how to get promoted or otherwise advance in your career, and last but certainly not least, how to manage the multiple priorities associated with being a working professional today.

In addition to my stories, advice, and occasional expert commentary, every chapter will include some fun facts, "Words of Wisdom" from other experienced executives, a "Survey Says" feature in which I highlight what current research has uncovered about the subject area, and a chapter summary that will help you put the material to work for you. And now, onward!

CHAPTER ONE

FIRST IMPRESSIONS: MAKE SURE THEY WANT TO SEE YOU AGAIN!

FAIR OR NOT, first impressions are critical when it comes to building a career because they are powerful and often difficult to change. So, we start here. Nothing can replace experience and a confident and positive attitude, but being judged on more superficial things like how you look and the way you speak are a reality of the working world. Approach your appearance as you would your resume. The most important part is the substance, but without clean formatting and proper spelling and grammar someone reviewing may never delve into the content.

YOUR DRESS IS A REFLECTION OF WHO YOU ARE

When I started working in an office in 1978, all the men wore suits and ties. If you worked at a serious company, like IBM, it was even more extreme: the shirt had to be white. Women wore dresses or skirts. You could wear dress pants if it was really cold or snowing, but you generally didn't. I don't mind getting dressed up, so for me this was part of the appeal of working in an office, but not everyone felt that way.

At the global market research firm where I've been working since 1983 and am now chief executive officer, we were early adopters of casual Fridays. But this was not a decision taken lightly. Many meetings were held, votes were taken, and memos were written. Since the term "business casual" was new, people needed guidelines about exactly what was and wasn't allowed (certainly no sneakers, shorts or dungarees, as we used to call jeans).

Notice the word "allowed." We were still in a business culture that was fairly authoritative. Management styles were just starting to change from the autocratic, top down, military style of the 1950s to the more modern, populist style promoted by leadership theorist Peter Senge. In his famous book, *The Fifth Discipline,* Senge encouraged companies to become learning organizations, where new and expansive patterns of thinking are nurtured and employee aspirations are set free. This was all fine and good, but it was still important to have rules and specific processes for monitoring and managing behavior. After all, what if someone dressed inappropriately? Who would address it, the manager or the Personnel Department (as HR was called back then)? What disciplinary action was appropriate?

In the 1990s, casual dress was a perceived employee perk that didn't cost the company anything. We moved from casual Friday to business casual all the time at the end of that decade, but jeans were still only allowed on Fridays. Personally, I held on to this one for a long time. In town hall meetings, we would often get asked about wearing jeans, and every year I'd say: "it's okay, but only on Fridays." And every year, they asked again. It was a standing joke.

Why were jeans so important to my employees? And what did I have against jeans? My rationale was that as a services company, we needed to maintain a certain level of professionalism and decorum—especially when dealing with clients. What if a client came to the office, or what if an employee needed to go to a client meeting unexpectedly? I also believed that if you dressed sloppily, your work and your attitude would be sloppy. Okay, and maybe I was still trying to hold on to a few of the precious rules that were in place when the baby boomer generation came of age.

It wasn't until my daughter Danielle got her first job that I had an epiphany. Danielle showed me that just because you *could* wear anything, that didn't mean you *would* wear anything—and many career minded individuals will use their judgment to dress appropriately, even if it's not dictated by a "rule." Regardless of gender, those that show up in flip flops, ripped jeans or tank tops are demonstrating they don't understand how to be appropriate in our work environment.

While there are many companies where it's okay not to dress up for an interview, you'd better know the culture and who will be interviewing you before you risk wearing something that could be deemed inappropriate. In my company for example, it is generally expected that men will wear a jacket and tie and that women will wear a nice dress or pants and a jacket.

A few years ago, we were looking for someone to fill an executive position that would report to me. The recruiter narrowed it down to two women, who were equally qualified for the position. One of the candidates came to the interview in a very low cut dress. Said dress was so distracting even one of the female interviewers said she had a hard time focusing on what the candidate was saying.

When debriefing about the candidate, we were all conflicted. She was clearly qualified, but we didn't know what to make of her choosing that particular dress for the interview. I called my mentor, an accomplished female executive who is on our advisory board to discuss the situation.

"I'm put off by her attire, but it's more about her motivation for wearing the dress than the dress itself," I said. "Why would she do this? Doesn't she realize the impact of her attire? Is she simply clueless, or did she wear the dress on purpose because she thought she'd be interviewing with men? What about the fact that the position reports to me, a woman? The dress was definitely a misstep, sort of like a man not wearing a suit and tie to an interview."

My mentor replied: "No, Karyn, you have it all wrong. This misstep wasn't like forgetting a tie; it was like a man showing up in bicycle shorts with his you-know-whats hanging out!" In the end, we all agreed. The candidate's attire demonstrated a lack of judgment, and we didn't want someone with poor judgment helping to run our company. We didn't hire her.

TAKE YOUR CUES FROM THE CULTURE

This was an example of where a first impression made a major difference in getting the job or not. And if you want to avoid making this kind of mistake, you have to dress the way that matters to the people who matter. However, it's not an exact science. Appropriate attire and presentation mean different things in different companies and industries. I have a friend who works for a tech company with a very relaxed environment in which the culture emphasizes being yourself and dressing comfortably. This means T-shirts and sneakers are the norm. She told me about a candidate who was dressed like an ad for Brooks Brothers and almost didn't get the job. You need to adjust your outfit to fit the situation.

If you're considering a new job, you'll also want to understand whether the culture is a good fit for you. You shouldn't necessarily have to hide who you are in order to get a job, but it might be hard for someone with blue hair and visible tattoos to be successful and happy in a conservative work environment.

Culture and context matter in other situations besides interviews. For instance, when our company acquired an outdoor sports tracking business in Colorado, the integration team advised me not to overdress.

"We want them to feel good about the acquisition," a team member told me. "Their outdoor sports culture is important to them and to our clients in that industry, so please assure them that we won't swoop in and change everything." I appreciated the feedback and adjusted accordingly, leaving my high heels at home in favor of a denim skirt and casual boots.

Occasionally, there will be snafus. I know someone who once showed up at a west coast technology company for a meeting. Her skirt and tights seemed like a great idea until her client announced that they'd be biking from one side of campus to the other. She managed to successfully get around without flashing anyone but was worried the whole time. Lesson learned: always wears pants when visiting Silicon Valley.

Words of Wisdom

"Always err on the side of professionalism in the way you carry yourself. It's never too early to begin honing your executive presence."

—Diana Schildhouse, senior vice president, Mattel.

LOOK THE PART

The good news, today there are many companies specifically looking for young professionals. They want fresh ideas, a youthful point of view, and technical skills young people can bring to their organization. They value youth. It wasn't always this way, and unfortunately, not every company is as progressive.

When I first started working, I was responsible for a large client account. My boss and I took the client out to lunch and somehow age came up. I freely offered I had just turned twenty-three, at which point my boss literally kicked me under the table! He later suggested I shouldn't let anyone know how young I was because it indicated I didn't have much experience. After that, I was careful to avoid mentioning age, to speak with confidence, and to dress in a way that conveyed poise and experience.

Recently, I was at a conference where a speaker presented on "Dressing for Success." Some younger workers felt they weren't being taken seriously when presenting to their clients or their leadership teams. The presenter encouraged the women to master important business skills AND consider wearing their hair up and putting on red lipstick to look older and more sophisticated. I'm not suggesting you run out and buy red lipstick, but do be aware of how dress and overall appearance can provide the illusion of a few extra years of experience.

Dressing appropriately is not just an issue for women. For guys, it basically comes down to tie or no tie, jacket or no jacket, and jeans or no jeans. When in doubt, it is generally better to go more formal than less. You can always take off your jacket or tie, but if you are in a T-shirt and jeans, there isn't much you can do to fix that.

Along these same lines, you may have heard or read the adage: "dress for the job you want." This means paying attention to how executives at the senior level or even just one level above you present themselves. Then, follow suit (forgive the pun). If you want to get ahead, give yourself a boost by appearing as the total package.

DID YOU KNOW?

In 1962, the Hawaiian Fashion Guild launched a campaign to make the iconic Aloha shirt (aka Hawaiian shirt) acceptable business wear. It argued Hawaii's hot climate made conventional business attire uncomfortable for most workers. The Guild took its cause to the state capitol, lobbying for government employees to be allowed to wear Aloha shirts every Friday. By the mid-1960s, people working at businesses across the state were wearing their splashiest Aloha shirts to mark the end of the work week. "Aloha Friday" was the precursor to what became "Casual Friday" in the mainland U.S.

NAMES AND THE HUMAN CONNECTION

Of course, once you get past the appearance hurdle, there's another important aspect of building an effective first impression—and that's establishing rapport. That means coming across approachable and finding mutually interesting things to talk about. The very first step in rapport-building is learning and then using a new contact's name. Dale Carnegie, the author of the famous business book *How to Win Friends and Influence People,* once said: "Remember that a person's name is to that person the sweetest and most important sound in any language." My mother is a master at this. Recently, my father was in the hospital. My mother knew the names of every nurse, doctor, and receptionist. It is amazing how much more accommodating people are when you call them by name.

Because using a person's name is also a great way of bonding with them, I take it very seriously. The key is to make it a priority when you are first introduced to someone. If you miss their name the first time, it is okay to ask again, but be sure to get it the second time.

There are some crazy techniques out there for remembering names, like Fred starts with an "F" and Fred looks like a frog and so on, but those don't typically work for me. My method is easier and generally more effective. I master names by saying them three times during an initial conversation: at the beginning, in the middle, and at the end. For instance, I might say: "Great to meet you, Fred," and then a little later in the conversation, "Fred, how long have you been with X company?" I'll end with: "I look forward to keeping in touch, Fred." This three-step process really works—give it a try!

I always ask whether someone prefers a nickname or I pay attention to whether he introduces himself as Mike or Michael. And if I'm not certain, I ask. I also check how to pronounce a name if it's unusual. Interestingly, people with unusual names are particularly grateful when you call them by their names since so few people do. In fact, if you ask, you may find that a person with an unusual name has a ready-made tip for remembering it. For example, I recently met a woman named Lassia. She quickly offered that it was like the famous TV dog, Lassie. In writing, I always find out whether a name is male or female and note how to spell it correctly. People view their names as integral to who they are, so using them effectively goes a long way.

When in doubt, err on the side of formality. I once had the opportunity to meet Leonard Lauder, who is a well-known leader in the beauty industry. A young colleague of mine and I were excited for the opportunity to discuss a business issue with him. We started our journey in an elevator to the 38th floor of the building where Estee Lauder is headquartered, where we enjoyed a magnificent lobby overlooking Central Park in New York City. From there, we were escorted to the executive lobby and then to Mr. Lauder's private waiting room. After we were invited to the expansive office of this beauty icon, my colleague burst into the room with an outstretched hand and announced: "Hi, Len!" I was speechless at this show of informality. Fortunately, Mr. Lauder was a gracious host, but in other circumstances, this situation might not have worked out as well.

WHAT'S IN A NAME?

It's common in most U.S. business settings to call people by their first names. In fact, this can help to establish you as a credible business colleague, regardless of your age or seniority. There are, of course, exceptions—like if someone is elderly, famous, or otherwise well-known. Realize too, that outside of the U.S., there are different customs. For example, in Germany and in many parts of Asia, people are often referred to by their surnames. When in doubt, be sure to ask.

GETTING TO KNOW YOU

When I meet new people, I also strive to find common ground quickly. I might ask about previous jobs, hobbies, family lives, and geographic areas, and when I was in sales, I even used index cards to keep track of my contacts. I put the name, company, and contact information on the front, and a few key details about them—such as a hobby or their children's name—on the back. If I knew I was meeting Pam, I'd pull out the card noting that she "has two kids and likes the Yankees." As an icebreaker, I'd start the conversation by mentioning one of those things.

Today, there are digital tools that make this process easier and allow you to share information with others as appropriate. But use caution and make sure your private musings about business contacts don't get into the wrong hands. When I was promoted to a sales manager, I turned my territory over to another salesperson. One day, she walked into my office, giggling. On the back of an index card, I had written: "Tall, cute and single!"

Even if a person is hard to get to know, it's worth it to find some type of connection. I once had an important client who was more reserved and it was hard to find a connection. I invited him to lunch and challenged myself to find a topic we could talk about. Finally, after trying many different subjects, I mentioned I knew sign language. That was it! He was fascinated, and as I taught him the signs for different animals and a few PG-rated curse words, we bonded. I wouldn't have believed it at the time, but sign language of all things was the catalyst for a long and mutually-beneficial business relationship.

SPEECH SHOULDN'T HAMPER YOUR REPUTATION

I'm not trying to sound like your mother, but watch how you speak. I know a woman who speaks like a Valley Girl. You know what I mean—like, *totally.* When I first met her, I couldn't believe she was as senior as she was. Once I started working with and got to know her, I realized she was incredibly smart and experienced.

Then, I started noticing her vocal imperfections less and less. But it took a long time to overcome that negative first impression based on her ditzy manner of speaking.

What you say is more important than how you say it, but just like with dressing, you don't want your communication style to get in the way of your content. While this is true for both men and women, women seem to get the brunt of the criticism. Much has been written about how women communicate and how it could be improved. In a recent article for *New York Magazine*, writer Ann Friedman listed a bunch of words and phrases women should avoid. The word "just" apparently sends a subtle message of subordination and sounds like you're asking permission. Be careful of saying you're sorry for things that aren't your fault. Don't use qualifiers like: "I'm no expert, but..." and don't turn declarative sentences into questions like: "I'll follow up the meeting with a status report?" Over at *The Muse*, Jennie Haskamp shared that women sound smarter if they eliminate emphasis words like "honestly," "absolutely," "really," and "literally." In terms of tone, women are instructed to watch out for vocal fry, which is that guttural growl that sometimes appears at the end of a statement, and you should also avoid my personal pet peeve, upspeak, which is raising your pitch at the end of a sentence. For the guys out there, you're lucky. People don't tend to criticize men's speech patterns or word choices as much. However, members of both genders should consider how to speak when meeting new people—but don't overthink it. After all, you want to sound like a natural human being, not a stilted robot.

FIRST IMPRESSIONS WHEN INTERVIEWING

When it comes to the importance of first impressions, the stakes are highest when you're interviewing for a new job. In addition to paying attention to your attire and image as discussed earlier, you'll want to prepare for the conversation. Everyone checks out the company website, but given the amount of information available online now, you're expected to dig deeper. Look at things like LinkedIn, blogs, and trade publications. If the company is public, you can usually read or listen to quarterly earnings reports. You should also be knowledgeable about the job for which you are interviewing, the people who are likely to be interviewing you, and the salary range for the position. There are many sites online that provide salary ranges for various positions.

Every interaction you have during the interview process—from your very first interaction—should exude confidence and the attitude that you deserve the opportunity. You may have seen the statistic that men apply for a job when they meet only 60 percent of the stated qualifications, but women apply only if they meet 100 percent of them. This finding comes from an HP internal study and essentially tells us that while men are comfortable selling themselves in the interview to make up for qualifications they may be lacking, women aren't. Realize that even if you don't have 100 percent of what they're asking for, you still might be the best person for the job and won't know unless you try. Focus on strongly communicating your accomplishments and experience and your genuine interest in the company and the position.

Words of Wisdom

"Create your own differentiated personal brand; one that will distinguish you from others. That's what makes you unique."

—Ivy Solowiejczyk, vice president, IBM.

Speaking of meeting people during interviews, let's talk about hand shaking for a minute. My parents were great mentors to my brother and me when we were growing up. My father felt it was important we know how to properly shake someone's hand so we would be taken seriously. As such, he taught us early the right way to shake someone's hand. We practiced with him and with each other until we got it right.

In the last few years, there have been a few articles extolling the virtues of eliminating the handshake and replacing it with the "Hey bro" fist bump pioneered by former President Obama. The fist bump has caught on a bit, but it does not and should not replace the handshake. For one thing, many people think it's ridiculous, and you don't want a new business associate's first impression of you to be that you're a buffoon. For another, using a fist bump risks offending a contact who expects a handshake.

It's amazing how many people who are new to business don't know the right way to shake hands. It's not hard. Look the person directly in the eye, give a nice, firm grip, pump once or twice and disengage. Women in particular sometimes have a soft or limp handshake or a half grip using more fingers than hand. These can create an impression of weakness instead of one of strength and confidence. If in doubt, check out YouTube for video instructions on the right way to shake hands.

What if you are under the weather? I was recently the keynote speaker at a conference with over 350 people in attendance. The day before the conference I came down with a very bad cold. The last thing I wanted to do was get everyone sick, but they were counting on me to present. When people came over to introduce themselves and held out their hands to shake, I put up my hands politely and said I had a bad cold and didn't want to infect anyone. Believe me, the attendees appreciated it. Along these same lines, it's also a good idea to carry a bottle of hand sanitizer and duck in a restroom to wash your hands periodically.

During an interview, in addition to shaking hands, most hiring managers will ask if you have any questions. To me, this is one of the most telling parts of the interview, and you will come across much better if you have thought about it in advance. I don't mind if someone brings notes: it shows me that they came prepared. The questions you choose to ask are important because they cement the strong initial impression you've been working so hard to establish prior to and during the interview. A simple online search will reveal dozens of potential questions to have in your arsenal, and most of the time, you'll want to stick with open-ended ones that are specific to the organization, company, or job. Also, steer clear of any questions that you could answer yourself with some brief research.

My favorite interviewee question is: "Can you share what it takes to be successful at this company?" Here are a few others to consider:

- What can you tell me about this job that isn't in the description?
- How would you describe the culture of the organization?
- What is a typical day like for a person in this job?

- What are the growth prospects for the person in this job?
- How is success in this job measured?
- Where do you see this team in five years? How about the person in this job?
- Is there anything that has come up in our conversation today or on my resume you would like more clarity on?

Once you brainstorm your interview talking points and potential questions, it's a good idea to practice. All the best entertainers and speakers rehearse a lot because they know it will result in a better performance. The more you practice interviewing—through role playing with family, friends, or career counselors, or simply by practicing aloud yourself—the better an impression you will make when it really counts. I used to play the "interview game" with my daughter. It was a fun way to build up her confidence in answering questions and it helped me practice my interviewing skills too!

Since jobs are not typically offered immediately after the first interview, the goal of that first interview is to get asked back for a second. Put your best foot forward even if you are not sure you want the job. That way, the ball is in your court to decide. A good way to usher that second interview along is to inquire about next steps. After you've asked your questions and are about to leave the interview, end with something like: "I really enjoyed learning about X job and am interested in exploring this opportunity further. What are the next steps in the interview process?"

Reinforce the strong impression you made in your initial interview by sending a thank you note immediately afterwards. I'm a big fan of handwritten notes (which we will discuss later), but after an interview, it is best to send an email since it's faster. Impress them with your promptness! If you interviewed with several people, send each one a personalized email based on the conversation. You might think a group of people in the same office won't take the time to confer on the content of a thank you note, but you'd be surprised. In my company, when several of us interview the same candidate, we always share the follow-ups. Copying and pasting stock language doesn't reflect well on you. Finally, be persistent. Some companies have a more buttoned-up interview process than others. While you don't want to be annoying, checking in once or twice about the status of the open position will show that you are interested and assertive enough to follow up.

SURVEY SAYS: FIRST IMPRESSIONS

I might argue first impressions are tough to change, but you don't have to take my word for it. According to recent research conducted by psychologist Vivian Zayas at Cornell University, people have a hard time getting over the first thing they observe about someone, and they're actually pretty good observations.

"Despite the well-known idiom to 'not judge a book by its cover,' this research shows that such judgments about the cover are often good proxies for judgments about the book—even after reading it," Zayas said.

Zayas asked participants to view a photograph of a person and make a snap judgment about how he or she would feel about that person if they interacted. About a month later, when the study participant and the person in the photo did interact, their predictions about how much they'd like the person were very accurate.

The idea that first impressions formed from physical appearance tend to be accurate is supported in another study published in the *Personality and Social Psychology Bulletin*. This research, conducted by University of California psychologist Laura Naumann, looked at the accuracy of observers' impressions based on full-body photographs.

Naumann and her colleagues concluded that both static appearance cues (e.g., clothing style) and dynamic appearance cues (e.g., facial expression, posture) offer valuable personality-relevant information—including how extroverted or religious a person may be!

Voice is critical for first impressions too. "From the first word you hear a person speak, you start to form this impression of the person's personality," said psychologist Phil McAleer at the University of Glasgow. His study recorded people reading a paragraph that included the word *hello*. After extracting all the hellos, McAleer had participants listen to the different voices saying the one word and rate them on 10 personality traits such as trustworthiness, aggressiveness, confidence, dominance, and warmth.

There was significant agreement among participants regarding the voices that were most and least trustworthy, most and least confident, most and least warm, and so on and so forth. And here's an interesting tidbit: what made women sound more trustworthy was whether their voices rose or fell as the end of a word. When women drop their voices at the end, they are showing a degree of certainty—indicating that they can be trusted.

CHAPTER SUMMARY

- Dress the way that matters to the people who matter. Understand the culture and who you're likely to meet before you risk wearing something that could be deemed inappropriate. Consider if there is anything about your appearance (e.g. tattoos, piercings, cleavage) that could potentially make a negative impression.
- Select attire that allows you to be yourself, while also fitting into your environment. Dress for the position you aspire to have, including clothing that's suitable for your line of work and appropriate shoes and accessories. Remember names by first making them a priority and then using them three times during an initial conversation: at the beginning, in the middle, and at the end.
- When meeting new people, find common ground quickly. Ask about jobs, hobbies, family lives, and geographic area. Jot down a few personal details to bring up next time. Invite the new person to tell you about him or herself and riff off their responses.
- Communicate in a way that builds trust and credibility. Avoid vocal imperfections like vocal fry and upspeak, and steer clear of words that undermine your confidence.
- Prepare for interviews by doing substantial background research and thinking through some intelligent, open-ended questions you can ask the interviewer. Create and practice talking points that relate the skills you have to what the interviewer is looking for.

CHAPTER TWO

NETWORKING AND RELATIONSHIPS: BUILD A FOUNDATION

I'VE ALWAYS VIEWED building business relationships like putting money in the bank. Every time you have a positive interaction with someone, you create equity. And this way, if something goes wrong down the road, you can make a withdrawal and still retain the relationship.

I had a client who worked at a major company on the West Coast. She was demanding and my team found her difficult. Since we are about the same age, and have similar interests like fashion and fitness, I used those to get her to open up to me over time. Once, she shared a personal situation about some challenges she was having with her son. Whenever we spoke after that, I asked about her son and how he was doing. As the years passed, he matured and became a real source of pride for her. She always lit up when she'd talk about him.

Recently, we were having an issue with a product this customer bought from us. My team was working hard to solve the problem, but she wasn't satisfied with the progress and was threatening to cancel the service. I flew to the West Coast in an attempt to smooth things over. I took her to lunch and to my surprise, most of the lunch was spent catching up on social matters. She wanted to tell me all about her son's new job and her plans for the summer.

Finally, toward the end of the meal, I raised the business issue. "Karyn," she said. "This is a tough situation, but I trust you and I know you will make sure your team fixes the problems as soon as possible." I am fairly certain that if it wasn't for the relationship this client and I had built over the years, my company would have lost the business.

Some people think that work is work and it's not important to bother building a relationship—that interactions can be strictly professional and transactional. You pay me for X and I deliver Y. I couldn't disagree more. So before we talk about how, let's talk about why. Here are just some of the benefits of building business relationships:

Revenue/Profit

- Easier to upsell.
- Fewer sales efforts.
- Less rework leads to improved margins.
- Referrals lead to more business.

Knowledge

- Learn more about the business and industry.
- Learn about competitive threats.
- Can provide a better product or service when you know what the customer wants.
- Can learn about opportunities for new product development.

Efficiency

- You know how they want things. Things run more smoothly with less effort and fewer mistakes.
- You are familiar with their business issues so you can better anticipate their needs.
- You know the shortcuts that will get the job done more quickly.
- You have more opportunities to correct or avoid problems.
- You know when a contact is crying wolf versus dealing with a serious issue.

Personal/Job Satisfaction

- Business contacts can become your friends.
- When trust is built, stress is less.
- Providing better service is more rewarding.
- Doing this well can provide additional career opportunities in the future.

KNOW WHAT'S HAPPENING IN YOUR CONTACTS' ORBITS

Although the advantages are numerous, building a relationship requires attention and effort. Previously, we talked about the importance of remembering and using names as well as establishing common ground and engaging on a personal level when you meet a new business contact. Even when you know someone well, you still want to do these things so you can continue to grow the relationship.

I don't want to reach out to my contacts only when there is a problem, so I often call to tell them a project is on schedule or to provide a piece of relevant business news and then make casual conversation. I'll do these calls on a Monday or a Friday. On Monday, I can ask about what they did over the weekend, and on Friday, I can ask what they're planning for the weekend. I've found this to be a very effective way to deepen the relationship beyond the business at hand.

And, as we discussed in the previous chapter, I strongly recommend you record these findings. After three dozen years in business, I've accumulated so many business contacts that there's no way I can remember all the details about everyone. As of late, I am a fan of Salesforce.com and I am diligent about making note of the interests and hobbies of my contacts and referring to them in future interactions. People really appreciate when you remember something like which college their son was trying to get into or the fact that they were going to Bora Bora on their honeymoon. Another favorite way to develop a relationship is to send someone an article or link relating to something that interests them (like cooking or dogs, for example). Finally, I love sending my contacts books—either digital or hard copy. I still remember being given a book called *Younger Next Year*, which was inspiring and relevant to people around my age. I ordered a stack of them: the book is now my go-to for reinforcing common ground with certain contacts.

I also like to acknowledge big milestones in my business contacts' lives. If I know, for example, someone got engaged, married, or had a baby, I'll send a physical card or a gift. If someone had an operation or an illness, I'll send a card or a gift basket. If the person in question is a client, it's often possible to expense these overtures, but I don't go crazy. Sending something extravagant when a client has a policy against accepting gifts makes everyone uncomfortable.

You can bolster business relationships not just by appreciating the more typical milestones, but by showing that you value what's important to the other person. If you work in the same building, you can learn a lot about a person based on what they have displayed in their cubicle or office. You might, for instance, find out a colleague is running a marathon and can ask about their training.

While we're on the subject of personal interests, if you're participating in an activity like a charity bike ride, you can encourage stronger relationships with your colleagues by asking for their support, but proceed with caution. I've found a good practice for doing this is to ask people with whom you have an actual connection, approach them infrequently, and make sure you have genuine passion for the cause.

ALL HAIL THE ICEBREAKER

Especially when the attendees of a meeting don't know each other well, I like to start meetings with an icebreaker in which we go around the room and introduce ourselves. We include name, position, and how long we've been with the company. But, in addition, I ask that everyone share a tidbit or fun fact. Usually, fun facts relate to hobbies, sports interests, or pets. If you have a veteran in the room who's done this before, have that person go first to set the tone.

If you don't want to bother with a fun fact, you can keep things simple with the basic: "where were you born?" People aren't put on the spot to come up with something clever, and answers always generate interesting discussion. Or, if you want to be more creative, you can ask people to name something on their bucket list, or the last app they downloaded. Whatever question you choose, an icebreaker is a great way to start the meeting off with a bit of fun and a more personal touch.

Lately, I've started snapping photos to reinforce a positive meeting. Regardless of how senior the people are, I've never had anyone balk at doing this. Afterward, I'll email the photo as a reminder of our meeting. A colleague of mine uses this idea too, but with a twist. When he occasionally takes someone to a special outing, he'll frame a photo and send it over. Clients love getting a memento of themselves at Fenway Park or the U.S. Open!

CONSIDER HOW YOU CAN HELP

Strange as it may sound, there's no better time to strengthen a business relationship than when a contact is not in a position to do business with you or is out of work and looking for a new job. I once had a client with whom I became very friendly. Over lunch, she told me she was going to quit her high-powered, high-paying position to run a winery in Napa Valley with her husband. I was shocked, but said I wanted to keep in touch. I insisted we meet again in six months so I could hear all about her new adventure. At this point, there was no opportunity for us to work together. However, we sustained the relationship, and then, one day, she told me she was done with the wine gig and moving to Asia for a new position. Her new company was one with which I was trying to do business, so she was one of my first stops when I went to Asia on a business trip. Sometime later, she was instrumental in helping my new manager in Asia become acclimated to the region. I know she valued that I kept in touch even when she wasn't a client of mine, and it helped deepen our relationship.

Similarly, if I can play headhunter for someone out of work by making a critical introduction or forwarding a useful lead, they're likely to be my friend for life. As an example, a client was let go as part of a big company restructuring. He had been a strong advocate of ours and I was sorry to see him leave. My team needed help on a short-term project, and I was able to offer him a consulting assignment while he was in-between jobs. It was a win/win. I filled a need in my organization and assisted a great contact until he found full-time work. He eventually found an influential position and became one of my most loyal clients.

Words of Wisdom

"Focus on being a good listener, which includes being patient and attentive. Equally important is to speak well, sincerely, and truthfully."

—Diane Bowers, president, CASRO.

THE BENEFITS OF FACE-TO-FACE CONTACT

Whenever possible, I try to meet in-person with business contacts. I'm a big fan of meetings over food. Offering to "grab a cup of coffee" or meet for a "quick bite" are good ways to do this informally. I'm a morning person, so I was doing power breakfasts before they were even a thing. In fact, more than once, I've had three breakfasts in one day! I often don't have a specific agenda for these meetings; my purpose is simply to deepen the bond with the other person and "put money in the bank." While we certainly may discuss general business issues, this is not the time for Excel spreadsheets or contract negotiations.

My daughter Danielle likes to bond with contacts in the form of "sweat-working," which involves business contacts going to workout classes like Soul Cycle or barre class together. Toronto-based productivity consultant Clare Kumar told *Fast Company* that after running with a former co-worker contact every Sunday for four years, that colleague became hugely helpful in launching her business and connecting her with media opportunities. Whether the goal is to land a new job or build rapport with a business partner, exercise can serve as a great equalizer. "There's no corporate armor on anymore," said Kumar. "You're in a more vulnerable place. Relationships can grow in a different way." A round of golf or a nail salon or spa visit are options too. There's something about hanging out with someone while lugging around clubs or wearing bathrobes that organically strengthens the relationship.

What are the best subjects to chat about in-person? This depends, of course, but there are a few topics that work well. Avoid religion and politics! I've had success with issues relating to people at the same life stage: for example, commiserating about the trials of college admissions, planning a wedding, or coping with the challenges of young children or aging parents. Or if you don't feel comfortable getting that personal, entertainment is a safe option. You'd be surprised how quickly a bond can form over a shared love for a movie or TV series. I have, for example, heard colleagues go on and on about Sunday night's episode of *Game of Thrones* on Monday mornings. After feeling shut out for months, I told my husband that it was a career necessity that we start watching it!

Words of Wisdom

"Realize early that doing great work and producing results isn't enough. Build broad relationships and high visibility."

—Terri Snyder, chief marketing officer, Checkers and Rally's Restaurants.

MAKE THE MOST OF NETWORKING EVENTS

Given my preference for connecting with people in-person, I attend many trade shows, conferences, and networking events around the world each year. Success in a networking situation is not about how many LinkedIn contacts I make but rather the quality of those connections. I'd prefer a few interactions that have the potential to be mutually beneficial. It's quality over quantity! In order to accomplish this, I try to find out who's attending an event so I can set up time with the people I want to meet. I then check bios and photos beforehand, which is now much easier thanks to social media.

A few years back, I had planned a dinner meeting with a prospect who we will call Bob Smith. We were scheduled to meet in the hotel lobby where our conference was taking place. We had described ourselves, but didn't share photos. I saw a guy standing around who matched the description, so I went over to him.

"Bob?"

He gave me a funny look and said yes.

"Hi, I'm Karyn," I said brightly, sticking out my hand. "How are you?"

"Great," he replied.

"Glad to hear it. Shall we go to dinner?"

He looked me up and down and said, a little too enthusiastically, "Sure!"

I finally said meekly: "Bob *Smith*?"

"No, Bob Jones," he said, disappointed. "Does this mean we aren't having dinner?"

In addition to previewing bios and photos, I also try to think about a few interesting topics in advance (industry happenings, current events, pop culture, etc.) so the conversation doesn't lag. This allows my contacts and me to get beyond the typical small talk about weather and where we live. During these initial networking meetings, my goal isn't to sell something, nor do I expect an immediate return. Rather, I want to get the person to a point where they want to have another conversation. I do this by being a good listener and showing genuine interest in the other person.

The benefits of connections made at networking events aren't always immediately obvious. Once, I was at a trade show in Las Vegas, I met Lois, a client, with whom I had a good chat. We discussed business and a common interest in helping women in the technology industry. She suggested I meet Carla, the founder of a women's technology association, and introduced us via email. Carla and I got together in New York City for breakfast and immediately hit it off. I told her about Mom.B.A., and she was intrigued. She asked if Danielle and I would speak at an upcoming conference. We were delighted to oblige and met dozens of interesting people there. During the speakers' dinner, I met Ann, with whom I felt a deep connection. As luck would have it, Ann was ideal to moderate a panel I was planning. Ann and Carla came to my event and met Dan, a colleague at my company. The story continues with Carla asking Dan to speak at a meeting in California where Dan met some retailers important to my company. While there, Carla suggested to Dan that he nominate me for an award, which I subsequently won! To bring this full circle, I invited Lois as my guest at the awards dinner.

I am especially mindful of time management at conferences and networking events. If my main objective is to meet and connect with certain people, I get to sessions early and leave the break time free for meet-ups. When possible, I prefer to plan exactly where to meet while onsite, so I'm not leaving it to chance. Networking can be hard if you aren't used to it, but like most things, it gets easier with practice.

At these types of events, I often get the chance to introduce my contacts to one another. Maximizing these interactions is an excellent way to build solid relationships all around. Instead of simply saying: "Lance, this is Maria. Maria, this is Lance," I'll share some pertinent details upfront. For instance: "Lance, this is Maria. Maria helped us with that research piece about sports trends. Maria, Lance manages U.S. marketing for Company X." If you are introducing an executive to a contact, mention titles. It will make the other person feel good that the CEO or president is taking time to talk to them, and the level of conversation is likely to be elevated as well.

I'm pretty good at names, but if I can't recall someone's name, I have a trick that usually works. It's great for social situations too, when people aren't wearing name tags. I use it a lot at weddings. I'll say, "Hi. This is my husband, Brad, or Hi. You remember my husband, Brad? Often, the other person will then introduce themselves to Brad, saving me the embarrassment of not knowing their name. What if you aren't sure if you met someone before? It's safer to say "so nice seeing you" than "so nice meeting you."

Strong networking involves timely follow-up. As soon as I leave an event, often on the plane ride home, I'll take out a stack of cards and handwrite notes to the key people I met. These are not generic "It was nice meeting you" letters. I make them personal and specific based on the topics we discussed, similar to an email you might send after an interview. Of course, these communications can be time-consuming, but they definitely stand out from the email clutter and help contacts remember me after a whirlwind of conference meet-ups. I will point out that my daughter thinks sending letters through the mail is old-fashioned and may not even get to your contact, but I still find it effective for networking purposes.

Often, I'll also follow up with LinkedIn requests to connect, and I always personalize those as well. I really dislike when someone tries to connect with me using the generic format, so I make an effort to do it differently. If I feel someone is important enough for a connection, then I owe them the courtesy of including a few relevant sentences.

DID YOU KNOW?

Social media usage is an ever-changing animal, but at the time of this writing, research shows it may not be the best way to network with senior leaders. According to a recent survey by MediaPost, just 30 percent of executive directors at the top 100 companies in NASDAQ are active on social networks. LinkedIn led the way, with 23 percent of executives maintaining a profile on the professional site, followed by Twitter with 11 percent. Eight percent of Fortune 500 CEOs have a Facebook account, putting them firmly behind America's grandparents in terms of adoption, and a little over two percent have Instagram accounts. Only 42 Fortune 500 CEOs have a Twitter account, though nearly a third hasn't posted anything in the last 100 days. Those who do post send an average of 0.48 tweets per day. Roughly half tweet once a month or less, and less than a quarter tweet daily.

YOUR NETWORKING COMMUNICATION STRATEGY

When I was starting out, there weren't many ways to reach people. For the most part, you called the person on their office phone line. Today, it's much more complex. There are tons of ways to communicate and everyone is partial to their own methods. For example, I find younger workers are generally more open to sharing their mobile phone number with all their contacts but until recently, I never gave my mobile phone number to business contacts. This is starting to change now that texting to coordinate travel and meeting times is more common, but I'm still extremely selective with who gets my number.

In addition to understanding how your individual contacts prefer to communicate, you should be aware of cultural mores within your organization and/or industry, and develop strategies for using various channels. It may or may not be appropriate, for instance, to text your boss to say you'll be late for an important client meeting. If in doubt, ask a more seasoned team member or mentor and be ready to evolve with the customs.

Words of Wisdom

"Build your network! Your connections, whether personal or professional, are the currency that will increase opportunity for your entire career. Learn the 'Give to Get' philosophy. Help those get what they are seeking. Adopt a mindset of abundance. The possibilities are endless!"

—Robert Fishman, partner, Sandler Training.

Professional social network navigation can be particularly tricky, especially for those not raised on the internet. I tend to use LinkedIn for business contacts and Facebook for personal contacts. However, this can get very confusing, especially if someone is both a friend and a business colleague. I often find myself asking "To Facebook or not to Facebook?" And on occasion I've tried to mix the two, and I've been a little hurt when company colleagues haven't accepted my Facebook friend requests. But then I try to remember that even though we are friendly, I'm still the boss and they might not want to open their personal lives to me.

I now understand how to adjust my privacy settings on Facebook so that different things can be shared with different people. If you tend to post a lot of personal photos on a network where you're connected with people you don't know well, this could be a good option. With many millennials and Gen Z-ers having five or more active social networks, it's valuable to consider a system for managing your various social profiles and using platforms for separate purposes. Regardless of the social network, it's unwise to make public something you wouldn't want your boss or a prospective employer seeing.

There are not many hard and fast rules for social media use, but remember that just because you are comfortable connecting and sharing on a certain channel doesn't necessarily mean your contacts are too—especially if they are from a different generation or different country. Be conservative in your initial outreach and don't take it personally if your contacts indicate they'd rather connect another way. And finally, if you are a baby boomer like me and don't have millennial offspring to advise you, adopt one as a reverse mentor!

SECRETS OF DAVOS

In a recent interview, venture capitalist and entrepreneur Rich Stromback told *New York Times* bestselling author Greg McKeown: "Opportunities do not float like clouds in the sky. They are attached to people."

Stromback is known as Mr. Davos, having spent the last 10 years attending the World Economic Forum in Davos-Klosters, Switzerland. "The forum is the most influential community in the world. It's the United Nations, G20, Fortune 500, Forbes List, tech disrupters, and thought leaders all brought into one," Stromback commented.

Stromback knows where the big events will be because he has so many people feeding him information, and he makes sure to be at the center of the action at Davos. When a Middle East Prince was asked to meet with some Fortune 500 CEOs, he reached out to Stromback to attend and facilitate the meeting; when the Vatican was trying to negotiate a peace treaty of sorts, it asked Stromback to help. What are his secrets for making the most of the Holy Grail of networking events?

"Ninety-nine percent of Davos is information or experience you can get elsewhere, on your own timeframe and in a more comfortable manner," Stromback told McKeown. "I don't go to sessions because that's not where the highest value is. What you can't get outside of Davos is the ability to have so many face-to-face interactions that either initiate or further key relationships."

This means knowing where people will be, and it may not be at the big-name parties if they're hosted at the wrong time in the wrong location. It also means understanding people at the highest levels of business and politics are hungry for real conversations and relationships that are authentic and sincere. "Nobody wants to have a 'networking conversation,' so I just put myself in the most target-rich area and then just go with the flow and spend time with people I enjoy," he said.

SURVEY SAYS: FACE-TO-FACE NETWORKING

You've probably heard the old adage: it's all about who you know. But there's a reason this wisdom has been passed down through the generations. According to a Right Management survey of 50,000 professionals, person-to-person networking is the single most effective way to find a new job.

Most research focuses on the type of networking that leads to the best opportunities, especially since, in the digital age, so much communication takes place via online and social networks. *Forbes Insights* recently found 80 percent of business executives prefer in-person meetings to technology-enabled communication. And Ivan Misner, the founder of BNI, the world's largest business networking organization, surveyed 12,000 global professionals and found people who get the most results from networking efforts participate in casual contact networks like a Chamber of Commerce, a referral network, or a professional association.

Why is networking still so powerful when we have so many other options today? Ed Keller and Brad Fay, co-authors of the book: *Why Real Relationships Rule in a Digital Marketplace*, have an answer.

"Face-to-Face conversations tend to be more positive and more likely to be perceived as credible, in comparison with online ones. The richest social gold mine is right under our noses: in the word-of-mouth conversations that happen in our kitchens and living rooms, next to the office water cooler, and on the sidelines of youth sporting events. These are the places where we actually live our lives," they said.

In addition to promoting more authentic interactions, face-to-face meetups apparently spur greater creativity. The Meetology Group's Laboratory on the show floor of the IMEX exhibition in Frankfurt was designed to answer the following question: "Does meeting face-to-face improve creativity in meetings compared to virtual meetings?"

Meetology Group psychologists conducted an experiment in which pairs of participants worked together on a creative problem solving task. Participants were divided into three separate conditions: face-to-face, video link, and voice only. They found the number of ideas generated, the quality of ideas, and the variety of ideas improved in the face-to-face condition over the virtual meeting condition. This raises concerns over the increase in remote workers, as being one and managing one are apparently more challenging.

Even as face-to-face interaction remains critical, our social skills are getting weaker. According to UCLA psychiatrist Gary Small, when the majority of your time is spent in front of a screen instead of talking with real people, it's harder to engage effectively when the opportunity presents itself. Since you want to be as confident as possible with managers, colleagues, and partners, the next time you're tempted to text or IM a business contact, force yourself to pick up the phone or set up a lunch date. You don't want to be out of practice when it really counts.

CHAPTER SUMMARY

- Building business relationships is like putting money in the bank. Every time you have a positive interaction with someone, you create equity, and if something goes wrong down the road, you can make a withdrawal and still retain the relationship.
- Be aware of, and make frequent reference to, the occurrences in your contacts' lives. Keep up to date by making occasional status calls during which you can then transition to casual conversation.
- Whenever possible, meet in-person with business contacts. Sharing a meal, exercising together, and discussing what's popular on TV are terrific ways to forge a bond that goes beyond business.
- Good networking is quality over quantity. Before you attend a networking event, find out who's going in advance so that you can set up time with the people you want to meet. Brainstorm a few interesting conversational topics such as industry or current events so that you are prepared.
- Strong networking involves timely follow-up. Communicate personally and specifically so you don't risk getting lost in a sea of conference meetups.
- Develop a strategy for each social network on which you are active, understanding exactly what you're going to share and with whom. Be conservative in your initial outreach and don't take it personally if your contacts indicate they'd rather connect another way.

CHAPTER THREE

SURVIVING YOUR BOSS: WE ALL HAVE TO REPORT TO SOMEONE

Adam was my manager when I got my first job as a project director in a survey research company. I was just out of college and didn't know anything about market research. He was the most nurturing boss you could imagine and was extremely kind and patient. As an entry level individual, most of my training was through hands-on, one-on-one, on the job training rather than formal classes. I sat in Adam's cubical, squished in against the wall next to him, as he showed me how to write questionnaires and analyze data. He was always supportive but he also provided critical feedback, when I needed it.

One day, I was writing a tabulation plan by hand, preparing data for delivery to our computer programmers. I found this kind of work easy and somewhat mindless to write. After completing the plan, I proudly showed it to Adam.

"This is very neatly done and your handwriting is perfect," He replied. "But the work is perfunctory. I don't feel you put any real thought into it. I know you can do better. Why don't you give it another try?"

Looking back, even though Adam's message was hard to hear, he was on target and shared his feedback from a caring place. A few months later, we were compiling the results of a Coke versus Pepsi taste test (yes, really!). I checked all the tabulations against the plan, made sure the numbers added up just right, and prepared to mail the final results to the client. Then, Adam asked me which brand had won. I was mortified. In my diligence to check all the numbers, I lost sight of the most important finding. Adam explained that while it is important to make sure the information is accurate, it's even more critical to step back and see if the data makes sense. I needed to be careful not to get stuck in the weeds, and, as they say, "miss the forest for the trees." Since then, I always make an effort to focus on the big picture and ask: "What?" (what are the facts?), "So What"? (what does it mean?) and "Now What?" (what should we do about it?).

In the 1980s, conventional wisdom said you shouldn't stay at your first job for more than two years. My father was a big believer in this, so when I hit that point he pushed me to move on. His theory was if you start somewhere as a junior person, people will never take you seriously. And as wonderful as Adam was, my dad was right. When I hit that two-year mark, I started to feel stifled. I had changed and grown, but Adam treated me the same. He still expected me to spend all my time with him. I wanted to make more connections with people, so I'd try to walk around and talk with others, but if I was away from my desk for a few minutes, he'd page me. I can still hear it over the loud speaker: "Karyn Schoenbart, please call extension 286." Adam was a micromanager who always had to know where I was and what I was doing. It was clear he wasn't allowing me to be more independent. Sadly, I realized that to keep developing, I needed to move on.

Adam didn't take my departure well. He was very hurt, and we lost touch. When I was working for him, I thought Adam was the best manager I could possibly have. But in retrospect, I think I was wrong. The best managers not only mentor and teach, but they also encourage their direct reports to grow.

In my next job, I worked for a small market research company that was expanding. I was hired because I had experience they were looking for to launch a new business. My office wasn't really an office at all—it was a warehouse where one of the owners (my boss) and I would work. After the new venture was up and running, we'd move into the headquarters with the other employees, but until then, my boss and I were on our own.

This was a completely different experience from the one with Adam. My new manager, Seth, had his heart set on hiring one particular person who used to work for him, but she was unwilling to relocate and reneged on the job. After working for Adam, who adored me, I was in culture shock with this new boss who barely even wanted me! Seth also had very little time for me, since it was just the two of us responsible for getting this venture up and running. He'd basically tell me what needed to be done, and I was expected to take care of it. Since he didn't have time to give me a lot of direction, I needed to figure it out on my own. It was the opposite of nurturing.

But here's the kicker: at this stage in my career, Seth's approach was exactly what I needed! After being micromanaged for so long, it was scary, but also liberating. I had to make my own schedule, determine how and what to get done, and most challenging of all, how to assess myself while my boss was busy doing more important things.

Today's twenty-somethings expect a lot of feedback because they are always striving to learn and grow. I felt that way too, but since I wasn't getting much input from Seth, what could I do? I had no choice but to figure it out myself and take ownership of my own development.

Lists became an essential way to manage my time. I'd learned from Adam to focus on the big picture and not just the small tasks. So, in addition to listing out daily tasks, I also set short, medium, and long-term goals to evaluate my progress. Since I was accustomed to constant feedback, this was a big change and a tremendous learning experience. It forced me to grow in a whole new way.

Who was the better boss, Adam or Seth? Adam was certainly more of a mentor and teacher. But as your career develops, you don't always need the mentor-manager. Sometimes, you need to learn for yourself. Throughout my career, I've had nurturing, involved managers, but I've also had hands-off ones. The truth is, both types are important.

Later in my career, I worked for a woman named Linda. She was a happy medium between Adam and Seth, a nurturing type that also supported me in expanding my responsibilities. We enjoyed working together for 15 years. While this was one of the more positive experiences in my career, I must admit I probably worked for Linda too long. There comes a point when a relationship gets stale and you need someone new to push you in different ways. When I switched divisions, and moved on from Linda, I was re-energized and my learning curve was steep but rewarding.

Words of Wisdom

"Just work really, really hard. It's amazing how good life is if you work hard. Second, set goals. Goals are free. Success is about staying hungry, and setting a goal is a way of creating hunger."

–Bracken Darrell, CEO, Logitech.

BE YOUR BOSS' RIGHT HAND

The best-case scenario is not just to survive your boss, but to get along with them. And the easiest way to do this is to ensure they like and trust you, and that they think of you first when important things need to get done. The perfect time to make this happen is early in your relationship. When you meet with a new manager for the first time, ask about their priorities and what they need to do in order to be successful in THEIR role. Based on what you learn, develop a plan for your contributions right away, and make sure your boss is aware of those contributions on their behalf. "Arm them with stats, soundbites, and other information to share with their boss and peers about what you've accomplished together," suggested writer Melanie Duppins at *CareerRealism*.

Don't assume you and your boss will "just figure out" the best way to work together. Ask early and often about their expectations of you and how you can communicate with them and deliver work most effectively. If you say you're going to do something, show you can be counted on without numerous reminders. Take on additional responsibilities without being asked, and when you receive constructive feedback, be grateful rather than defensive and work to incorporate it immediately.

You don't have to be best friends to be your boss' right hand. But if you don't respect them, that will show and is a recipe for disaster. How do you get around this? *CareerRealism's* Duppins provided this advice: "Create a sincere one sentence response to the question, 'What do you most admire about your manager?' Have that response handy, and find a way to use it when asked about them and their skills. You'll find that telling others what you like about them makes you believe it more. As a bonus, if your manager hears that you've been spreading praise about them, it can't hurt your relationship!"

Finally, loyalty goes a long way. Don't complain about your boss when they aren't around, have their back in politically-charged situations, do your best work even when no one's looking, be consistent in your behavior, and don't give ultimatums or threaten to leave. All these things will help you build a reputation as the person on your team your boss can rely on the most.

SUCCEEDING WITH REMOTE MANAGERS

Especially if you are new to a company or to a position, and you aren't yet experienced in your role, being separated from your manager by geography can be very challenging. I once met with the summer interns at my company to see how the internship program was going. Two of them were struggling with remote managers who were very busy. Given this style of work is increasingly common, what's the solution?

My bosses have always been local, but I've managed remote employees and it works best to establish the rules of engagement upfront—make sure you and your manager decide how and when you are going to communicate. Email and a quick phone call may work for day-to-day issues that arise, but also build in regular, one-on-one touch bases too. I like to do these via Skype or another video method so I can see the person for a better connection. In preparation, collaborate to develop an agenda so each of you has the chance to cover the issues most important to you.

During meetings, don't be tempted to multitask. Give the person your full attention and turn off your devices and email. Use these check-ins as an opportunity to be transparent about what's really going on. Bad news doesn't get better with time, so be prompt about communicating any problems and remind your boss about your accomplishments as well. When you hang up, be proactive about summarizing the meeting in email. And finally, seek out opportunities for in-person contact whenever possible and remember the tips from Chapter Two on building a bond. You can "put money in the bank" with a remote manager just like you can with a colleague or client.

DID YOU KNOW?

History is full of less-than-stellar bosses. One extreme example was 19th-century railroad baron George Pullman, whose company manufactured sleeping cars. According to *Mental Floss'* AJ Jacobs, Pullman built an Orwellian town for his workers to live in, complete with schools and a church, but no fun stuff (like taverns or non-sanctioned newspapers). His inspectors would march into homes to make sure they'd been properly cleaned. Pullman even replaced American currency with Pullman money so he could control the prices of food, rent, and supplies. As one unhappy worker put it: "We are born in a Pullman house, fed from the Pullman shops, taught in the Pullman school, catechized in the Pullman Church, and when we die we shall go to the Pullman Hell." When workers staged a strike in 1894, Pullman refused to negotiate, and the crisis spiraled, leading to gunfire and the deaths of several workers. And you thought your boss was a control freak!

NOTCHES IN THE BELT

Although it can be uncomfortable, you can learn as much, and sometimes more, from a bad boss than a good one. I'm not talking about someone who is abusive, which is inexcusable. I'm talking about a manager with a style you might not appreciate at first. When managers are more junior and in the process of developing their own skills, they don't always make the best bosses. This was true for Danielle as she was starting her career, so I told her that these tough experiences were notches in her belt. The more notches she got, and personal experiences she had to draw from, the better manager she would ultimately become. Most people who have been in business a long time will have sub-optimal managers at some point. This isn't always the worst thing. When you experience different approaches, you begin building your own view of how you want to manage. Then, if you become a supervisor yourself, you can select the aspects of previous managers that best gel with your own style. You choose those you want to emulate versus those you want to avoid. The more varied management experiences you have, the more you can empathize with your own direct reports and develop into a well-rounded leader.

BUT I'M WORKING FOR THE DEVIL!

So, what if your manager is *really* bad? First, make sure it isn't you. I once heard a comment that if you think all your roommates are jerks, then maybe you're the jerk. If you think all your managers are bad, take a careful look in the mirror and make sure you aren't the one with the problem. For example, if every supervisor you have had micromanages you, then perhaps you aren't demonstrating that you are on top of things and can complete a project autonomously. Or, if you feel none of your managers give you enough feedback, maybe you are coming across as defensive.

If you are sure the issue is with your manager, the first step is to talk with them directly. It is best not to do this when you are angry or upset. In the past, I found it helpful to make a list of everything that bothered me about my boss. When I stepped back and reviewed the list, I realized many of the things were petty and that I'd have a better outcome if I focused on the one or two most important issues. I wrote out my talking points and practiced them, and then asked for a private meeting in a quiet place to voice my concerns. I was careful not to make the conversation about the things my boss was doing wrong, but rather stayed focused on how the situation made me feel. People will be more willing to listen to what you have to say if it doesn't come across as an attack on them.

You are also more likely to make progress if you are specific about what you would like to see happen. For example:

- "Robert, I know sometimes my work needs improvement and I'm eager for your feedback, but when you criticize me in front of my peers, I'm very embarrassed. I'd appreciate if we could schedule one-on-one time instead so that I could fully focus on what you are suggesting. Would that be okay with you?"
- "Marla, as you and I have talked about, one of my goals is to be more assertive in meetings. I am working on this. However, in two recent meetings, I felt that I didn't get an opportunity because most of the questions were directed toward you. Since this is an objective of mine, can we work to find a specific part for me in our next group meeting?"

Assuming you have tried to talk with your manager directly about the issues at hand, but things are still not improving, what do you do? Sometimes it just requires patience. I was once moved into a lateral position as a stepping stone to a much bigger job. During this phase, I reported to Mark, who was not a very good manager. He was awkward and had a hard time connecting with people. He ran a big group and I was asked to work for him so I could learn that business. It was a bit hard on my ego, but I was pretty sure it was temporary and basically had to suck it up. I wasn't negative, and I didn't speak badly of Mark to my peers. I did whatever I could to demonstrate my own leadership skills by taking on special assignments and projects while connecting with other company leaders. In the not-too-distant future, I was able to move on.

If you have a bad boss, don't let your discouragement affect your work. Especially if you like the company, you want to shine so there is no question you are an employee worth retaining. I would not have been promoted out from under Mark if I let my disappointment with the reporting structure get me down. Why sabotage your success by slacking off? Instead, understand what your goals are and keep a record of how you're progressing relative to these goals. This will give you a platform to showcase your achievements in discussions with the HR department and other senior people in your company.

OTHER FISH IN THE SEA

If your manager can't or won't be your advocate, others may be willing to step in. This is one reason why you should build your internal network before you run into issues and regardless of whether your manager is good or not.

Danielle has done this brilliantly. In every role, she has built strong relationships outside her immediate team, talking with senior leaders in good times and in bad and sharing her progress toward her goals. She established a rapport so if she got to a point where she was eager for a new challenge, she could raise it with her confidants and they would view it in the context of her as a valued employee.

We will talk a bit about mentors and sponsors later, but relationships like Danielle's don't have to be in the guise of a formal partnership. In fact, many of the best mentoring and sponsoring relationships develop organically. These relationships can be built on some of the concepts we talked about earlier, like getting to know someone and finding common interests, but they should also develop because these senior individuals have come to appreciate your work ethic and capabilities. Look for people with whom you have had an opportunity to connect on a project or assignment. Today, there are an increasing number of matrixed management relationships, so you may be able to tap other senior people besides your boss who reside in your business circle. If you have proven yourself to be a valuable contributor that the company does not want to lose, they could serve as allies in issues with your direct manager.

There is a fine line here. You don't want to come across as whiny or unprofessional, and your goal should be to honestly seek advice on how to deal with a difficult manager. If you decide to broach the topic, do it in a private space. Talk about the business' needs without badmouthing or gossiping about your manager. Here are a few ways to potentially start the conversation:

- "Bob, thanks for taking a few minutes to talk with me. I know you have worked with Adam for a while and I was hoping you could give me some advice on how to engage most effectively with him. I've been here for about two years and I would like some additional independence, but I'm having difficulty getting Adam to let go. Do you have any suggestions for what I might do differently?"

- "Diane, I really like it here, but I'm struggling a bit with how to best work with my manager, Susan. I want to do my best, but I can't seem to get enough of her time to review my work. I know how busy she is, and I don't want to come across as too needy, but I am worried that I'm not delivering the best product for the customer, especially when I get the feedback from her after the fact. Do you have any thoughts on the best way to remedy this? If Susan doesn't have the time, is there anyone else you could recommend who I might be able to run things by?"
- "Debra, I think you know from our work together on X project that I'm incredibly dedicated to this company and I don't mind working hard, especially when we have a time-sensitive project. But lately, I'm concerned Jane's expectations are beyond what I am comfortable providing on an ongoing basis. I've been getting emails and calls very late into the evening and frequently over the weekend. One of the things I like about this company is our culture and how we respect people's personal time. Has this changed in other departments or is this unique to Jane? I don't mind working crazy hours on a short-term basis, but I don't want to get burned out. What are your thoughts?"

I should warn you this strategy can backfire if not handled well, especially if your boss finds out. This is why you want to make sure you have a solid working relationship with the person you approach and you have already exhausted other options including discussing the issues with your boss directly. Remember, the point is to further develop this person as your ally and engage them as a sounding board. On one hand, you may get some useful advice that will allow you to re-engage with your manager and work things out. On the other hand, your ally may already know this manager has issues, and now you've made them aware there is a serious concern. Either way, ask your adviser if you can touch base again in a few weeks.

If you have proven yourself as an asset to the company by doing exceptional work and going above and beyond, hopefully the higher-ups won't want to lose you. Then you can safely engage in a discussion about how to improve the situation. It might result in a new opportunity or manager. If others have similar issues, the manager may be moved out of their role.

One thing I should point out: if you have a serious problem with your manager that involves sexual or racial harassment, abusive behavior, or substance abuse, this issue should be brought to HR immediately and not discussed with others in the company. It's HR's job to identify an effective (and legal) way to resolve the situation.

Words of Wisdom

> *"You never get what you don't ask for; as long as you approach people with respect and a sense of partnership, ask for help and you will be amazed what happens."*
>
> *—Oliver Libby, chair and co-founder, The Resolution Project.*

WHEN IT COMES TO BOSSES, ALWAYS BAD TRUMPS SOMETIMES GOOD

As reported in *Inc. Magazine*, research conducted by Michigan State University and published in the *Academy of Management Journal* set out to uncover which employees have the less fortunate scenario, teams led by straight-up jerks or those helmed by unpredictable loose cannons. Apparently, people employed by erratic leaders have it worse.

The researchers separated subjects into two groups and asked them to play a stock-pricing game. One group's members played the supervisor and the other's members played the employee while the researchers monitored participants for an elevated heart rate, a sure sign of stress.

If the study subject playing the supervisor provided fair feedback, unsurprisingly all was well. But when the boss was unfair, things got interesting. It turns out having a boss who is consistently unreasonable and nasty raises stress levels less than having one that swings between behaving like a decent human being and being a complete monster.

"Our findings essentially show that employees are better off if their boss is a consistent jerk rather than being fair at times and unfair at other times," commented lead author Fadel Matta. "Inconsistent treatment is much more stressful than being treated poorly all the time." Sadly, this makes sense. At least if your boss is always obnoxious you know what to expect.

AVOID FUTURE BAD BOSSES

Once you've had one bad apple, you're motivated to do everything in your power to avoid another one. Fortunately, you don't have to leave this up to chance. When interviewing with a new company or department, do your research ahead of time to make sure you're not getting into another situation with a less-than-ideal manager. Check out their LinkedIn profile first, looking for a stable job history and positive recommendations from direct reports. Then, even if you interview with HR, you should always insist on meeting the person who will be your direct supervisor. In-person is best because you can learn a lot through body language and general rapport. Putting aside the fact that you're in an interview situation, does the potential manager put you at ease? When you imagine working with them, are you more enthusiastic or fearful?

Try also to have coffee or lunch with one or more staffers at the new company. Ideally, these individuals would be in a similar role and in the same location, reporting to the same manager. On paper, your purpose is to learn about the organization and its culture. However, you can also use this opportunity to discover as much about your potential boss as possible. What you don't want to do, however, is go overboard. You don't want to come across as a stalker! Information about your new boss' personal life, for example, is not relevant. Simply ask team members a few innocuous questions about how they like working with this manager and how the manager has helped them achieve their goals, and then read between the lines. If team members brightly and earnestly sing the manager's praises, this is a good sign. But if they look like they are struggling to avoid saying something negative, that's a red flag.

SURVEY SAYS: WHAT MANAGERS WANT FROM EMPLOYEES

It's easier to have a good relationship with your boss if you understand their expectations. Surprisingly, the top qualities managers look for in their employees haven't changed much in the last 50 years. In a recent study, Karin Helgesson at the University of Gothenburg in Sweden studied the most frequently requested employee characteristics in recruitment ads. She found that the ability to cooperate, personal drive, and the ability to work independently appeared fairly consistently through the 50-year period. However, since the turn of the century, personal drive has displaced ability to cooperate as the No. 1 requested characteristic.

In a second study conducted by American Express, researchers interviewed 1,000 managers from a variety of American industries and companies to determine what today's leaders want to see from their best employees. Eighty-seven percent of managers said because they now have to do more with fewer resources, the ability to prioritize work is the most important skill they are looking for in employees. Eighty-six percent of managers are looking for team players who are willing to share credit and help out when necessary. In terms of how they want to communicate, 66 percent of American Express' manager respondents prefer in-person meetings, while 32 percent want to hear from you over email. Despite technological advances like Skype and Slack, face-to-face time remains critically important to establishing a strong manager/employee relationship. And finally, most managers want what's going to make YOU happy and help YOU grow. Seventy-three percent of managers said they were willing to support employees in changing roles within the organization if the move would help reports meet their goals.

Employees often need to rely on studies like this, because sadly, the vast majority of people lacks a clear idea of what their managers expect. In a Florida State University study published in *Business News Daily*, less than 20 percent of employees said they were certain they knew what was expected of them at work each day, with the majority reporting varying levels of clarity concerning responsibilities, ranging from "some" to "complete" ambiguity.

The study, which assessed the opinions of more than 750 employees across multiple job environments, uncovered a number of significant differences between those who knew what was expected of them and those who didn't. Specifically, 60 percent of those uncertain about their responsibilities reported higher levels of mistrust with leadership, while 50 percent had higher levels of overall work frustration. In addition, 40 percent felt they were being overworked, while 33 percent were more likely to search for a new job within the next year.

Most respondents cited a lack of leadership as the reason responsibilities were unclear. Specifically, employees said managers fail to be forthcoming and proactively develop communications until a lack of accountability triggers an organizational crisis. And these accountability problems cost American organizations hundreds of millions of dollars each year in both direct and indirect costs.

CHAPTER SUMMARY

- As your career develops, you don't always need a mentor-manager. Sometimes, you need to learn for yourself. Depending on your unique stage, either a nurturing, involved supervisor or a hands-off one might be more important.
- Build a positive relationship with your boss based on mutual respect and trust. If you aren't getting along, carefully consider if you might be part of the problem. Then, give your boss a chance to help you resolve it by approaching them directly.
- Bad bosses are like notches in your belt. When you experience different approaches, you begin building your own view of how you want to manage. Then, if you become a supervisor yourself, you can select the aspects of previous managers that best gel with your own style.
- If you do have a bad boss, don't let your discouragement affect your work. Instead, understand what your goals are and keep a record of how you're progressing relative to these goals. This will give you a platform to showcase your achievements in discussions with senior leaders in your company.
- It's a good idea to proactively establish relationships with senior executives who you can turn to advice or support. Look for people with whom you have had an opportunity to connect with on a project or assignment. If you have proven yourself to be a valuable contributor who the

company does not want to lose, they could serve as allies in issues you are having with your manager.

- Do your best to avoid future bad bosses. Even if you interview with HR, you should always insist on meeting the person who will be your direct supervisor. In-person is best because you can learn a lot through body language and general rapport.

CHAPTER FOUR

MANAGING AND MOTIVATING OTHERS: STEP AWAY FROM THE DESK

Early in my career I was in a sales role, and I discovered I was good at it. Success in sales generally requires you enjoy helping people, are willing to work hard, and are motivated by results—so this was a natural fit for me. After a few years in client service, I switched companies and joined a new firm as a salesperson. At the time, there was a contest in place where anyone who saw 130 clients in-person during the quarter won a prize of $1,500. I started a couple of weeks into the quarter, so I had to see an average of 13 clients a week for 10 weeks to hit the target.

I still have my 1983 planner showing all my meetings. I was a road warrior. It was a challenge, but I was determined and eventually won the prize. More importantly, all those sales calls paid off and I beat my revenue target for the year. The more companies I saw, the more proposals I wrote, the more contracts I sold. The formula for success was clear and within a few years, I'd been promoted to manager.

While sales came easily, management did not. Aside from bossing around my younger brother when we were kids, I had no experience and no training. In the early days of my new role, I didn't change my day-to-day job very much. I retained most of my clients, but now also had to "manage" all these other people who were reporting to me. When one of my direct reports would come into my office and sit across the desk, all I could think was: *how can I get this person out of here as quickly as possible so I can get back to my real work?* Hitting my personal sales quota was still my top priority.

Within six months of my new assignment, the company conducted a review in which people evaluated their managers on a long list of criteria such as: *Makes me feel like an important member of the team; Because of him/her I'm better at what I do; Takes time to understand what I want in my career.*

When I received my results, I learned I was in the bottom quartile of all the company's managers. I was devastated. I'd prided myself at being the best at whatever I did, and I certainly wasn't the best manager. Apparently, I wasn't even a good manager. I was also conflicted. A major decision presented itself. Was I serious about being a manager, or should I go back to being an extremely effective individual contributor?

I reached out to different people for their input. One leader I respected asked me how important it was to make an impact on the company. "Look, Karyn, even as a top salesperson, the most you're going to generate is about one million—maybe two if you have a fantastic year," she said. "But if you can develop a sales team that's as good as you are, then you'll generate tens of millions. Your value to the company will be exponential."

The decision came down to this: if being successful based on my own performance mattered most to me, then I should stay in sales. However, if it meant more to have a broader impact on the company, then I should take the more challenging job, stretch myself, and learn how to be a sales manager. I chose the latter and started making changes.

An American Management Association course helped change my orientation from "all about me" to "all about the team." I met with my reports and owned up to my management flaws. I shared my commitment to changing the way I worked with them. Next, I moved a small table into my office so that when I met with someone, I could literally come out from behind my desk and leave my own work to focus on them. The small act of sitting side-by-side is an approach I still use to this day. I also scheduled a brainstorming session in which I asked everyone to talk about the impediments to achieving their goals. I told them how important it was for us to all be successful and asked that they not hold back. We filled the white board with issues and concerns. It was amazing how satisfied they felt after this opportunity to vent.

I, on the other hand, felt horrible at first. I had a stomach ache just looking at the long list of challenges on the board, but then I realized this was my roadmap to making improvements. I prioritized the list and systematically eliminated the barriers one-by-one, all the time communicating progress to my team members. Gradually, as they realized I could be trusted to do what I said, they began to see me as their advocate.

Then, I did the hardest thing of all. I let go of the last of my personal clients and my own quota. My success was now fully dependent on my team members meeting *their* numbers. This was scary, but it also meant I was really a manager now.

Soon enough, I was up for another manager review. I scored much better this time, moving from the bottom quartile to the top. I was thrilled, of course, but I was even more excited that my team exceeded its revenue goals that year. It has been 30 years since that first sales manager role, and on my road to CEO and through the many teams with whom I've had the pleasure of working, I've picked up many strategies for managing and motivating employees that lead to positive business results and high company morale.

I place great importance on cultivating relationships with my employees and ensuring they are engaged. I believe the secret to strong team morale is to make its members a top priority. I write this into my business plan and make employee satisfaction and morale part of each manager's evaluation. Putting it in my plan and on my agenda lets my team know this is important to me.

When I ran my first business unit, my motto was very simple: Keep Staff Happy, Keep Clients Happy, Keep the Company Happy. The first two lead to the third. If you do right for your people, then they will do right for you.

THERE'S NO SUCH THING AS TOO MUCH COMMUNICATION

As a leader, it's essential to be a clear and consistent communicator. When I became a new manager, I tapped into my strong communication skills to ensure I was listening to the needs of my team. I also made sure my team understood the broader company vision, where they fit, and how they could help achieve it.

Today, I try to avoid the pitfall of communicating everything via email. I believe we rely on it too much, so I use different vehicles for different purposes, such as in-person meetings, conference calls, video chats, webinars, etc. For more serious matters, in-person contact is best, as we will discuss in the next chapter.

If you are lucky to have your team in one place, you can set up a central command center where you post information and gather for impromptu meetings. When I ran my first business unit, we were all housed in the same location. I went out and bought a big, brass ship bell to hang on the wall in a central location. Every time someone received a new contract, they would ring the bell and the team gathered in front of it. The person who made the sale would describe to everyone how they pulled it off, and we would clap and give our congratulations. The process took just a few minutes, but it provided a nice boost to the whole team.

Regular team meetings are a great opportunity to communicate and engage employees. I always have an agenda and start and end on time. One of my bosses was fond of saying that if you are five minutes late for a meeting and there are 12 people in the room, then you didn't waste just five minutes, you wasted an hour. I follow a simple plan for meetings: "Tell, Do, Tell." Tell them what you are going to do, do it, and then tell them what you did. Many managers forget the final step, but it's crucial to remind people of progress. Back when I had the long list of challenges from my sales team, I was diligent about providing updates so my people knew the issues were taken seriously and were being addressed. I'm convinced this was a big part of how I gained their trust.

In these meetings, I also include agenda items that allow team members to actively participate by sharing their experiences with others. It could be something they learned at a training class or at a conference, or it could be a success story regarding a sale or internal efficiency. Sometimes, I invite guest speakers from other parts of the company to broaden the perspective of my team.

Many years ago, I started a "Kick Off the New Year" meeting. This has since become a widespread practice at our company. It's an opportunity to review the previous fiscal year, celebrating the successes and honestly assessing the misses. We share the objectives for the coming year, starting with the overall corporate plans and how the team's goals fit into the bigger picture. Time permitting, a kickoff meeting is also a good time for a training or team building activity. Finally, we take advantage of having everyone together to welcome new hires, congratulate people who were promoted, and recognize personal milestones like engagements, marriages, and new babies. These types of recognition don't need to wait for the annual meeting, though. You can use them in any group gathering.

I also like to host a meeting at my house from time to time. While still a business meeting, it is a much more personal and intimate way to interact with my team. My direct reports like this so much they have started taking turns hosting the group at their homes. One person with an apartment in New York City had everyone over for cocktails and a city view, while a suburban resident served up pulled pork on his outdoor barbeque.

Words of Wisdom

"Early on in their careers, every young manager should embrace collaboration and the value of diversity, and in a completely selfless manner, leverage these to power their careers."

—Linda Todd, director, Category Marketing, Walmart.

SKILL DEVELOPMENT: TOOLS AND TRAINING

Just like you wouldn't build a house without a blueprint and the proper wood, nails, and a hammer, you can't expect employees to be effective without the right tools and skills. I often ask people what they need to help them do their jobs well. One of my favorite questions is: "If I gave you a magic wand, what would you want to help you do your job?" I recall an instance in which an employee eyed my office printer enviously and admitted his team's hallway printer was always busy with a line of people waiting for their documents. How inefficient! I picked up the phone, and the very next day, that team had a second printer. One of my employees once said: "Our leaders have big scissors and will cut through red tape if they can—you just need to ask." A printer sounds like a small thing, but often small things add up and go a long way to solidify healthy relationships and improve productivity. If the request is a more significant investment, I ask the employee to provide a short business case demonstrating the ROI (return on investment). This is a good way for someone to articulate the business need, and if it's compelling enough, I oblige.

Too often people think of training as an obligation when they really should think of it as a privilege. Training is an investment in the employee. There are all kinds of formal trainings available, but informal opportunities can be just as effective. For example, when I ran a client service team that presented to customers a lot, we created a practice presentation process. Whenever someone had an important external presentation, they booked a conference room and invited the whole team (including people in other functions such as operations, marketing, and finance) to attend a run-through. These weren't mandatory, but most people liked to go. The presenter went through their deck from start to finish, without interruption. At the end, everyone provided feedback on the content, the slides, and the delivery. Since the goal was to provide the client with the best product possible, input was constructive and there were never any hard feelings. Of course, the presenter benefited from the practice, but the attendees benefited too. People behind the scenes got to learn more about the business, and the operations folks could see firsthand how their work contributed to the end deliverable.

I also love the concept of "Lunch 'N Learns." We pick a topic, assign someone or a group to develop the content, bring in some pizza, and have a session. It's a great way to get people together and have those with knowledge about a topic share it with others.

Creative, on-the-job training ideas can come from anywhere. I encourage people to come up with their own ideas and give them a try since there is little to lose. Over the years, we've done things such as "A Day in My Shoes," where people spend time shadowing someone in another function; "Crossing Borders," where teams present what they do to other groups, and "Birds of a Feather," where people with similar positions in different divisions get together to share common issues and learnings. When I was in sales, I started an audio club, which was like a book club with audio tapes. Since we were in sales, we were on the road a lot, so I ordered a bunch of sales training tapes, and we'd take turns listening to them. Then, we'd meet (over pizza, of course) to discuss how to apply the concepts. It was fun and educational, and those tapes sure helped pass the time on long drives alone.

Whatever their function, top performers are usually eager to learn. They are hungry to be a part of task forces or committees, attend trade shows or conferences, and get their hands on special projects or assignments.

Of course, skill development should take place in the broader context of the company's needs and then tie to an overall development plan for the employee. What are the person's career goals, what skills do they need to achieve them, and what training is required? Setting short and long-term objectives provides a road map and allows you to check progress.

GETTING OFF TO THE RIGHT START

Some of the most critical decisions I make on a regular basis involve hiring. I recognized early on that when you're building a team, you want people with skills which complement yours. People new to management/leadership tend to hire "mini-mes." As tempting as it is to work with someone who thinks just like you, it is not nearly as productive as having different points of view on your team.

In order to get a balance of skills on the team, I'm strategic about interviewing. First, I make sure everyone doing the interviewing is prepared to ask a different set of questions. We usually convene to share our reactions. When there are multiple interviewers, though, it's necessary to avoid groupthink. A friend of mine told me about a method her company uses to prevent this. Each person who interviews the candidate writes down a numeric score on a scale of 1-10. Outliers express their opinions first.

The period after immediately hiring a new employee is crucial, and yet many supervisors fail at this. Think about this from the employee's perspective. Can you imagine starting a new job, not knowing where to go, getting to your desk, and having no supplies and no one to welcome you? Believe it or not, I've heard stories from people who have had these experiences. What a missed opportunity! Making a new hire feel welcome is one of the easiest ways to get off to the right start.

HR often has a formal onboarding and orientation, of course, but leaders also have the responsibility of creating a positive first impression and experience. New hires should have their name on their workspace, their supplies waiting for them, a welcome card from the executive team, and an appointment scheduled with HR for a more formal onboarding session. At my company, we also assign a buddy who can show them where things are and answer any questions. When feasible, their department head personally welcomes them and makes sure someone is available to have lunch. Even if your company doesn't have a robust HR department, there are small but impactful things you can do as the new person's manager: for example, you could prepare a small welcome kit with a list of "who's who" and some background about the company and their department.

I once led a task force to develop an onboarding program, and in researching best practices, there were two key findings that stuck with me. First, most people will learn more from meeting with other people than from reading information in manuals or from a company intranet. So, a hallmark of our onboarding is to provide a list of key people for the employee to meet with in their first few weeks. The other finding? Most companies do a good job of onboarding in the first month or two, but that's all. Therefore, we try to spread out onboarding activities over at least six months.

Even for the most senior new hires, I always put together a list of short-term objectives that focus on learning the new job. I typically schedule weekly one-on-ones to ensure the new hire is on track with their onboarding plan, and I'm diligent about providing feedback on milestones after 90 days. I have found the more time I invest upfront, the quicker the employee will be self-sufficient and able to contribute at their full potential.

Finally, at my company, we schedule regular new hire breakfasts with company leaders and mid-level employees who have been with the company for a while. During the meal, we go around the room and have each person say the department they work in, where they worked before, how they found us or how we found them, and a fun tidbit about themselves. Mid-level individuals also share their career trajectories and what has compelled them to stay with us. These breakfasts are a great way to get to know new employees and show we value them as people.

Words of Wisdom

"There will always be someone who can benefit from your experience, so lean in and help others to be successful so the circle of success grows."

—Hana Ben-Shabat, partner and board member, A. T. Kearney.

FEEDBACK AND PERFORMANCE EVALUATIONS

Employees, especially younger ones, want and need regular guidance from their managers. According to a TINYpulse survey, nearly half of millennials expect it once a week—twice the percentage of every other generation.

As a manager, it is my responsibility to help my team members be the best they can be. This means I must occasionally provide critical feedback, but it doesn't have to be hurtful. I was once told by an employee I didn't provide him with enough constructive criticism. I responded: "Yes I do, Rob, you just don't realize it." After all, the objective of feedback is to change someone's behavior, and if that is accomplished, the person doesn't need to feel bad about it.

When you give feedback from a caring place and your people understand you sincerely have their best interests at heart, they will respond better to constructive comments. Timing is also important. While immediate feedback is ideal, remember the goal—help them be the best they can be. I prefer not to approach people when emotions are running high—negative or otherwise. For example, I once watched a talk in which the speaker, who was one of my direct reports, was holding a glass of water the whole time. While her content was terrific, I felt the glass was distracting, and it took away from her ability to gesture to make specific points. I wanted to mention it to her but she was so pumped up after her talk I decided to wait until just before her next presentation. At that point, it was easy to simply suggest she leave her hands free to punctuate her talk. Mission accomplished with no hard feelings.

Constructive feedback is a bit of an art. I always avoid giving it to an employee in front of other people, and I keep the end goal in mind. I focus on the other person and how to best communicate with them, not what is most comfortable for me. For example, I once had two employees, Pete and Liza, who both needed coaching on their attire (yes, it's that topic again!).

Pete had recently started a diet and exercise regimen and lost a lot of weight. He looked great but continued to wear his old clothes, which hung on him and looked sloppy. Knowing Pete is always seeking and open to feedback, I was comfortable telling him it's terrific he's gotten so much healthier, but it's time to go out and treat himself to some new clothes that fit better.

With Liza, it was much more sensitive. Liza tended to dress like she was about to go to a club: she looked fashionable, but it was too revealing for the workplace. We struggled with who should talk with her: her manager, HR, or me. I decided to take it on, since I had a mentoring relationship with her and could address it constructively. I started with a compliment about how well Liza was doing and congratulated her on a recent promotion. I suggested this new promotion presented a good opportunity to elevate her image. I asked her to look for other women leaders she admired and use them for inspiration. Unfortunately, this subtle approach wasn't enough, and I had to be more specific. Liza was very surprised as she thought she looked "nice." I agreed she did, and then said while she should maintain her own style and individuality, she might want to tone it down for a more professional look.

This feedback involved a version of the "sandwich approach," which means you start with a positive comment, add a negative one, and end with another positive one. I have used this technique very effectively over the years, although new literature indicates it may not always be the best strategy. A lot depends on the employee, how senior they are, and how well you know them. I once had a senior direct report resign because he was moving to Romania as part of a major lifestyle change. At our goodbye lunch, I asked him for some feedback on my managerial style. He said: "Karyn, you know that sandwich thing that you do when giving feedback? Well, especially with someone very senior, just go ahead and give the feedback—they can take it."

When it comes to evaluating employees, formal reviews have been the norm for decades. However, in addition to the annual review, good managers provide specific, fair, and accurate feedback regularly so anything that comes up in the review isn't a surprise and has already been addressed to some degree. There is a widespread movement right now to radically change the formal review process in favor of more frequent, continuous methods, which we'll talk about more at the end of this chapter.

However, assuming your company still does traditional annual reviews, be sure to supplement them with more agile, just-in-time feedback. People's goals should be clear and updated if they change. As a sign of respect for the other person, I always do both official and unofficial reviews on time and allow plenty of opportunity for discussion. Today, with so much being done via matrixes, a person's success depends on their ability to work effectively with colleagues. When a formal process for soliciting peer feedback isn't in place, I proactively seek it out so reviews are balanced.

I try not to be nitpicky in review situations. If someone is uncomfortable with how I've worded feedback, I'm willing to adjust it. As long as they get the point and change their behavior accordingly, I'm satisfied. I often discuss long-term career aspirations and am candid with the employee about their readiness for the next step. Finally, I usually close constructive feedback conversations by asking the person what I can do better as their manager and what they need from me to be successful.

Every now and then, an employee won't address performance feedback and will fail to improve. Letting someone go is never easy, and I get through it by carefully preparing documentation, practicing what I'll say, and keeping the actual interaction short. I do try to give people the benefit of the doubt, and I always confer with our HR team about proper protocol. However, I've found, more often than not, people (myself included) don't fire unproductive or insubordinate employees quickly enough. One of my smartest bosses once told me it's rare to regret your decision to fire someone, so, as unpleasant as it is, get on with it.

DID YOU KNOW?

People don't leave companies, they leave bad bosses, right? According to recent research published in the *Journal of Personnel Psychology,* this isn't necessarily the case. In a study of 700 employees at a multinational IT firm, University of Illinois management professors Ravi Gajendran and Deepak Somaya found, surprisingly, employees leave good and bad bosses at almost comparable rates.

The research proceeded like this: after assessing the leadership quality of each manager at the company, the researchers waited 18 months and then investigated which of the survey respondents had left the organization. While interviewing these 128 individuals to find out why they'd left, Gajendran and Somaya discovered good leadership doesn't reduce turnover because supportive managers empower employees to take on challenging assignments. Such experiences set them up to be strong external job candidates.

However, former employees with good bosses are what the researchers call "happy quitters," meaning they continue to have positive feelings toward their former employers and tend to stick around as active alumni—becoming sources of valuable information, recommendations, and business opportunities down the road.

MAKING PEOPLE FEEL IMPORTANT

Surveys of younger workers always indicate they overwhelmingly prefer managers who listen. Over the years, I've realized when I solicit ideas and feedback from employees on decisions that affect them, they feel valued. If I can let them vote on an issue, I do so, and if the situation is not a democratic one, I'll say that upfront. Even in these cases, I still want my team to be involved. I've learned that people appreciate knowing who will make the final call, so they aren't surprised if you go a different route. I make sure everyone feels their opinion is heard and we take time to discuss alternative viewpoints before moving forward.

If I ask for ideas via email on topics like competitive responses or efficiency opportunities, I always thank each person individually for their contribution—even if I don't plan to use the idea. This takes more time, but I value input and the last thing I want to do is discourage someone from contributing their thoughts.

If you can involve your team in the business planning process, that's an excellent way for them to feel ownership and accountability for the organization. For example, having select team members help plan an offsite meeting is an opportunity for them to be involved in something beyond their day-to-day responsibilities. For less experienced employees, it can be a chance to showcase their leadership abilities and contribute creative ideas.

I've used breakouts in which members of my staff split into groups of fewer than 10 people and go to separate locations to work on, for instance, a SWOT analysis (strengths, weaknesses, opportunities, threats). Some advance consideration should be given regarding the participants in the various groups—for instance, do you want everyone from the same function in a group or do you want to mix it up? I have at least three groups on a topic so when we share the results, there's enough input to identify common themes. I either assign a leader to each group (which saves time) or let the group decide. The basic idea is to brainstorm as many ideas as possible and then narrow it down to the top ones, and it may take some re-tooling before you master a method that works well for your team. My company, for example, once had a tradition in which the newest person would present the breakout group results to the larger audience. We considered it a rite of passage and a good way for them to get exposure. After a few years, though, we decided this was a mistake. New employees often didn't understand the nuances of the concepts discussed or have the broader context. Putting them on the spot in such a public way was unfair to them and not the best reflection of the group's work.

As a manager, you must be discreet about confidential or sensitive news. I have learned nearly everyone has at least one "best friend", and even if someone promises to keep your secret, they often don't. When sensitive issues like an organizational change arise, I provide timely information to everyone affected. I might even work with my fellow executives on a playbook of who's communicating what and when. The last thing I want is for someone impacted by a change to hear about it third hand or through the grapevine. This takes extra work, but it is part of making employees a top priority.

MOTIVATING YOUNGER WORKERS

Driven young professionals are often criticized for changing jobs often, but it's a misconception they embrace change more than members of prior generations. Rather, millennials more often leave jobs because their expectations of meaningful and challenging work have not been realized.

According to a study by the Center for Generational Kinetics and Barnum Financial Group, 60 percent of millennials stay at a company because the work gives them a sense of purpose. In *Harvard Business Review,* Tracy Benson shared the powerful example of General Electric's Ecoimagination Nation initiative. Over the course of three years, 8,000 GE employees—including a large portion of the company's young professionals—engaged in community volunteer activities that reduced greenhouse gas (GHG) emissions by 31 percent and water use by 42 percent.

In addition to promoting purpose within their organizations, the most effective leaders of young workers understand the need to develop a risk-tolerant culture that values innovation and experimentation. In response to millennials' entrepreneurial spirit, GE Global Research has launched an Open Innovation initiative aimed at creating a more dynamic, transparent forum for ideation.

We can also motivate young workers by appealing to their status as the first digital natives. Millennials are on the cutting edge in terms of adopting workplace technology that makes their jobs easier and facilitates collaboration with colleagues near and far. Benson at *Harvard Business Review* cited companies such as IBM, ADP, Ingersoll Rand, and Novartis as among the first to embrace digital communication systems like Yammer, Jive, and Slack, which provide real-time, ongoing feedback and dialogue.

Finally, millennial-savvy leaders appreciate young workers who crave new experiences and seek different types of rewards for strong performance. PepsiCo, for instance, now uses a lattice career architecture that allows employees constant access to opportunities for growth and skill acquisition and does not require they pursue a traditional upward path.

ACKNOWLEDGING PEOPLE, CELEBRATING SUCCESSES, AND BEING HUMAN

Mark Twain once said: "I can live for two months on a good compliment." Praising people should be soon, sincere, and specific. The praise will have a much bigger impact if you say something individual, such as: "Jessica, I was very impressed with how you helped Company X determine the right pricing for their new product. The client told me they are taking your recommendation to the CEO. Great work!" Compare this to: "Jessica, nice job last week."

According to psychologist Gerald Graham at Wichita State University, personal thanks rates number one as a motivating technique in the workplace, yet nearly 60 percent of employees say they don't get it. Frankly, I don't understand this. It isn't even about being nice—it's simply good business! Once you decide praise is important and should be a priority, the ideas are practically endless. There are so many ways to acknowledge employees that I could fill this whole book with them. I've also learned that whatever you do, change it up from time to time or it gets stale. While some people insist on monetary awards, a lot of research indicates recognition is more important and memorable than money. My favorite ways to acknowledge employees include:

- Company-wide awards for big achievements:
    - "Award for Excellence:" a quarterly incentive based on excellence over time. A committee reviews nominations. Recipients receive a financial reward, recognition on the company intranet, and their names on a plaque that is prominently displayed.
    - "What You Do Matters" Award: a small, monetary award that comes with balloons and a banner. Anyone can put in a nomination, as long as it's approved by the recipient's manager. When recipients move their workspaces, they often take the banner with them because they are so proud.
- "Hall of Fame:" I set up a "halloffame" email address where anyone can submit a client compliment. I regularly review the messages and send a personal email acknowledging the compliment and how the employee helped our business. Recipients are acknowledged on the company intranet.
- "Pass It On:" If I see good work, I ask the person who did it to send it on to others. Sometimes, I'll pass it on myself with the person and their manager copied.
- "Shout-Outs:" These are the easiest of all. Many groups do them at their monthly team meetings, simply allotting time for informal praise acknowledging a co-worker for something special they did.

In addition to personal recognition, there are lots of fun ways to celebrate team successes. Food is always a good motivator. Bringing in donuts or snacks as a way to celebrate an accomplishment is often appreciated. As I've mentioned, I love to acknowledge business successes and personal milestones like promotions, work anniversaries, and birthdays, and I've been known to be a bit sneaky about it.

In one instance, I called a two-hour meeting on a summer Friday afternoon. You could tell everyone was dreading it. I stood at the front of the room and announced gleefully: "We just had our best revenue month ever! Dump your laptops; we're going to the beach!" We threw a bunch of inflatable beach balls into the room to kickoff the surprise and headed down the block for an afternoon of fun. Although, I should point out that when Danielle heard this story, she didn't appreciate it. She said getting a mysterious invite from a senior executive makes people nervous. So if you want to try this, maybe tell your people upfront the gathering is nothing to worry about!

Other light-hearted ideas include a baby picture contest, a chili bake-off, and a pumpkin carving contest at Halloween. I don't always know what people will find fun, so I've launched committees staffed with volunteers who like planning these activities. Sometimes I'll give these self-dubbed "Spirit Committees" and "Sunshine Clubs" a modest budget or they will collect money from team members.

As you can tell, not taking myself too seriously is a core part of my managerial strategy. People need to see that I'm human. I love pink, and I'm not afraid to show my "girly side." One year, we were having a kickoff meeting on Halloween in one of our remote offices. The team working on the meeting decided everyone should dress up in costume. When I was picking my outfit, Danielle suggested I wear my pink jacket and pink shoes and go as Corporate Barbie. I smiled and said I would, but I was concerned they wouldn't realize I was in costume. Danielle laughed and said that was the point! I went for it, and my colleagues and employees enjoyed the costume and the back story.

Regardless of how you do it, make acknowledging people, celebrating successes, and coming across as an authentic human being key components of your leadership plan. If some of this doesn't come naturally to you, that's okay. Team up with people who do it well and empower them to help you.

SURVEY SAYS: EMPLOYEE ENGAGEMENT AND THE MANAGER'S ROLE

Several studies have illustrated that a majority of global workers are disengaged at work, and obviously, managers are a major factor. Gallup's latest report, *State of the American Manager*, provided an in-depth look at what characterizes great managers and examined the links between talent, engagement, and business outcomes such as profitability and productivity. The research showed that managers account for as much as 70 percent in variance in employee engagement scores!

If great managers seem scarce, it's because the talent required to be one is rare. Gallup's research revealed that only about one in 10 people possess the talent to manage. Though many people are endowed with some of the necessary traits, few have the unique combination of all the skills needed to help a team achieve excellence. However, an additional two in 10 people exhibit some characteristics of basic managerial talent and can function at a high level *if* their companies invest in coaching and development plans.

Gallup also found individuals who work for a female manager were six percentage points more engaged, on average, than those who work for a male manager. Female employees working for female managers had the highest engagement (35 percent engaged), while male employees working for male managers had the lowest engagement (25 percent engaged).

Employees of female managers outscored employees of male managers on 11 of 12 engagement items on Gallup's 12-item employee engagement survey.

Putting the gender issue aside, what else can we do to improve engagement? Regular recognition is critical. A study by research firm TINYpulse demonstrated that a significant majority of employees (79 percent) "don't feel strongly valued for the work they put in." The survey uncovered a strong relationship between how valued an employee feels at work and the likelihood they would re-apply to their job.

The way employees receive feedback from their managers also greatly impacts engagement. Based on multiple internal and external studies showing the yearly performance review and single ratings to be ineffective, technology company Adobe took the plunge and stopped using annual stacked rankings. In the 18 months following Adobe's announcement that it would replace the rankings with more fluid and contextual methods of differentiating performance, the company reported huge spikes in employee engagement and a 68 percent increase in share price.

The business world was blown away by these results and the agile performance management trend accelerated. Consulting firms Deloitte and Accenture, global health services client Cigna, and even GE—the company that once popularized the idea of forcing people into a performance curve—all announced changes to their performance management systems. By the time of this writing, hundreds of large firms were in the process of moving to a no-ratings system, and thousands more were reconsidering how they manage and evaluate performance.

CHAPTER SUMMARY

- The secret to strong team morale is to make your employees your priority, even writing people-related actions into your business plan.
- After making a new hire, you as the leader have the responsibility of creating a positive first impression and experience. Send a personal welcome card, assign a buddy, and take them to lunch. Brainstorm short-term objectives that facilitate learning and provide a list of people for the new hire to meet.
- Just like you wouldn't build a house without a blueprint and the proper wood, nails, and hammer, you can't expect employees to be effective without the right tools and skills. Ask people what they need to help them do their jobs well. A great question is: "If I gave you a magic wand, what would you want to help you do your job?"
- When delivering constructive feedback to an employee, focus on the method that will be best received by the recipient. Do not deliver criticism in front of others, wait for an opportune time, and communicate how and why you have the person's best interests at heart.
- More than anything else, employees want managers who listen. Don't just ask people for their opinions, beg for them and say thank you. When you solicit ideas and feedback from employees on decisions that affect them, they feel valued.

- Praise should be soon, sincere, and specific. The comment will have a much bigger impact if you say something customized to the individual.

CHAPTER FIVE

DEALING WITH DIFFICULT SITUATIONS: WHEN THE GOING GETS TOUGH, GET SMART

EVER SINCE I REALIZED I wanted to be a teacher, I've loved imparting information and knowledge to others. Today, I take the time to teach several classes at my company. These are very interactive and based on actual experiences. Two of the most popular ones are *Building Relationships* (101) and *Dealing with Difficult Client Situations* (201). The first course is usually a prerequisite for the second, but by reading Chapters One and Two you'd be able to skip right to 201!

In the *Building Relationships* session, I ask the participants to share examples of times in their lives when they received excellent customer service. Interestingly, over a third of the examples start with a negative experience. To reinforce this, I always read the following story from the *Pryor Report Management Newsletter*:

When a corporate executive was asked by a consulting team to name the company to which she was most loyal, she told them it was her hairdresser.

"Why is that?" the consultants said.

"Well, because the first time they colored my hair, it turned out green instead of blonde. They spent the entire day fixing it until it was right. They even paid my parking ticket."

The consultants asked: "Did it ever occur to you that they were incompetent?"

"No." She seemed surprised at the question.

Let me illustrate a bit more what I'm getting at here. The Jeni's Splendid Ice Cream brand is synonymous with "making people feel good." And in the spring of 2015, customers definitely didn't feel good after an outbreak of listeria. The company immediately pulled products from shelves, halted production, and responded by acknowledging the situation and taking responsibility. Jeni's CEO, John Lowe, was forthcoming and transparent, releasing a statement about how they were finding the root of the problem and preventing these situations from occurring in the future. The company backed up its commitment by testing every batch of ice cream before it left the facility, and managed to catch a second outbreak of listeria before the ice cream reached customers. Jeni's also set up a communications center to provide customers, partners, and the media with ongoing and timely information about the outbreak. The trust-inspiring communication and action Jeni's took during this crisis engendered worldwide respect and helped the brand gain traction.

Whenever I am dealing with a conflict or a negative interaction, I keep in mind that most people won't remember the actual issue, but they *will* remember how it was handled. A colleague told me years ago about a big disaster with a client. Her boss said "the place where the break heals is stronger than the arm was before," and she should use this problem to forge a better relationship. In fact, a favorable outcome can result in a closer relationship because bonds are often formed by going through a tough time together.

Nevertheless, it's still best to avoid problems in the first place. Whether you're dealing with an external customer or an internal colleague or manager, you can use the following strategies to prevent conflict.

Words of Wisdom

"Many things will happen in your career that are out of your control. How you respond to them will determine your future success."

—John Brown, manager, Corporate Market Intelligence.

AVOID POTENTIAL MISUNDERSTANDINGS

Clear communication is key to avoiding conflicts. I often witness people using ambiguous language that sets them up for a dispute. A phrase such as: "I'll have that to you the week of June 1," for example, is a recipe for trouble. The recipient interprets this to mean "She'll have this to me by Monday, June 1st" while you are probably thinking you have until Friday, June 5th. Similarly, what does "end of day" mean? Is it 5:00 p.m. or 11:59 p.m.? What if you are in New York and they are in Los Angeles? Does end of day mean your day or their day?

I'm guilty of using the word "hope" as in "I hope I will be able to get you an answer by Monday." The other person doesn't hear "hope," they hear "Monday." Other words that can create misunderstandings include "report," "topline," and "summary."

I've been burned by something as simple as providing a PowerPoint deck when someone was expecting an Excel spreadsheet. Now, I aim to be very specific when describing a deliverable, and when feasible, I show an example or template to ensure we are squarely on the same page.

I'm compulsive about putting things in email, especially if I've had miscommunications in the past. Most people today don't have time to read, so I keep written communication concise. If more detail is required, I'll include an executive summary at the top of the email to reiterate the key points, such as what was agreed to by when, and who is doing what. After the initial confirmation, I'll send regular progress updates so my boss, client, or team knows where we stand—especially if we are dealing with a situation that could become difficult.

Just because everything is eventually confirmed in writing doesn't mean you have to start there. In-person interactions have a much better chance of success because you can read the person's body language in addition to hearing their words. Your message is more likely to be well-received if you can match the style of the person with whom you are interacting. Regardless of whether they are no-nonsense and like things short and to the point, if they prefer a lot of background information, or if they need to chit chat before getting down to business, try to mirror their behavior.

KNOW YOUR BUSINESS—AND THEIRS

Another way to avoid problems is to be well-informed about the business issues at hand. There are many ways to learn more about a business, such as reading trade journals, following appropriate industry leaders on social media, reading or listening to quarterly earning calls for key companies, and talking with others who have worked on the business for a while. Once you have a good grasp of the business issues, you can avoid problems through what I call the "sniff test." If something doesn't quite seem right, it probably isn't. Trust your judgment and double check.

Additionally, ask questions to ensure you are digging deeper and not doing things just because someone said so, or because that's the way it has always been done. Educate others if you are working on something complex so there aren't misunderstandings based on a lack of knowledge. For example, when I sign on a new client, I take the time to walk them through the contract so they know exactly what is included and what isn't. This way, we avoid having to give work away for free later in the assignment.

LET THEM EMPTY THEIR GLASS

Despite our best efforts, "stuff" happens. Thankfully, in my business difficult situations don't come up too often, but I've seen my fair share. I've faced issues such as late or wrong information, clients who didn't like results even if they were correct, problems with a piece of software, or complaints about our pricing or billing. Then, there are the clients who want free information, demand the impossible, try to get their way by being bullies, are non-responsive, or play gatekeeper without letting us get to the actual users of our information. The list goes on! I regard all difficult situations as having a beginning, middle, and end. From the minute the problem is identified, my job is to ensure that I get through these phases as quickly and professionally as possible, keeping the issue contained and not letting it blow out of proportion.

What do you do when someone calls or approaches you and is very upset or angry? While it's important to address the issue, there's more to it than that. When my son Eric was in grade school, he had a teacher who wasn't a good fit for him. As a result, he was becoming very frustrated with school. I knew most of the teachers and felt that next year he should get Mrs. U, who would be ideal for Eric.

Just like I would in a business situation, I prepared a comprehensive list of grievances and arguments to make my case. I even practiced my speech. When I walked in to meet with the principal, how do you think I would have felt if she said, "Hello Karyn. How are you today? By the way, Eric is going to have Mrs. U next year."

Yes, this is a trick question. On one hand, getting what I wanted, I should have been happy. On the other hand, I would not have had the satisfaction of sharing my built-up frustrations and concerns about my son's education. Sometimes, just getting your way isn't enough—you need to be heard.

Imagine a glass completely full of water. If someone is upset or angry, until they can empty out some of that water, there is no room for anything. In other words, until they can get their points off their chest, they won't be able to hear what you have to say. The best thing you can do in this situation is to listen and then listen more: probing and asking questions until they have completely emptied their glass. During this kind of discussion, I always take copious notes so I can capture everything they said. Then I paraphrase back: "What I heard is..."

In a group meeting in which many people are disgruntled, you might use what I call the "talking stick" approach. Let me explain.

When Eric was eight years old, he was invited to a party with a Native American theme. The boys slept in a real teepee tent, listened to stories told by a member of a local tribe, learned and celebrated authentic traditions. Eric came home with a talking stick. According to historians, the talking stick has been used in many Native American traditions for centuries when a council is called. The talking stick is passed from person to person, and only the person holding the stick is permitted to speak. No interruptions are allowed. This was a big hit in our household because it allowed each family member to express their points of view before someone else could chime in. You don't have to have a talking stick per say. In fact, my family members will pick up the nearest inanimate object and claim, "I have the talking pen/brush/glass" to ensure they can speak freely. It is a good strategy to make sure everyone present has a chance to share their thoughts and feelings about a conflict.

TAKE CHARGE OF THE SITUATION

In a difficult situation, I don't rush to apologize until I know all the facts. I might empathize with a comment such as: "I hear how upset you are," and then add what I've found is an extremely powerful statement: "I will do everything I can to help resolve this as quickly as possible." Note I haven't promised I will give them what they want—but I have offered my assurance I am committed to a resolution. Another helpful phrase is: "Our relationship/partnership/friendship is very important to me, and I will make this my top priority."

Unless the problem is a simple one that can be solved on the spot, I prefer not to stretch for a resolution during this first conversation. I want to be able to gather all the relevant information and make sure I'm ready to put my best foot forward. And in general, it's not a good idea to provide too many solutions before someone asks. One of my employees, for example, once gave away free data to make up for a client issue, when the client really wanted a single report. The latter would have cost our company a lot less, if only we'd taken the time to hear her out!

After listening to everything the person has to say, I'll immediately schedule the next interaction. I do not want to leave this meeting to chance, and I certainly don't want to try to resolve the situation in email. While text and email are very efficient communication modes for everyday interactions, these are not ideal when faced with a difficult situation. It is important to have a two-way dialogue so you can respond in real time to objections or concerns. You want to be flexible during the discussion with replies that may differ based on the direction of the conversation.

Depending on the severity of the scenario and logistical issues, the follow-up can be a call, a videoconference, or an in-person meeting. Calls should be scheduled with a specific date and time, as in: "I will get back to you tomorrow morning with an update. What time is good for you?" I prefer to be the one making the call as it puts me in control and shows I'm taking charge.

The time between the initial conversation and the next conversation is the chance to gather information, using your notes to guide you. What are the details? What will it take to resolve the issue? How long will it take to resolve? Who needs to be in the loop? Should this be escalated to a more senior person? It's also the time to brainstorm solutions and think through options.

If you do not have the answers you need in time for the follow-up call, make the call anyway and schedule another conversation. Again, you don't want to make the situation worse by missing opportunities to communicate. Be honest but confident, as in: "Your business/our relationship is important and this issue is complex. I don't want to give you wrong information. I need more time to gather all the facts. When would be a good time to reach you tomorrow?"

GIVE BAD NEWS GRACEFULLY

Delivering bad news is never pleasant, regardless of whether it's a situation where someone reached out to you, or whether you have to proactively tell another person something they don't want to hear. Tempting as it is to hold off and wait for a miracle, your best bet is to get it over with quickly. If you're nervous, think about this: in the future, people will remember how you handled the situation more than what occurred. And, keep things in perspective. Someone I know once said that unless you are a doctor, a pilot, or the Secretary of State, it is unlikely that your problem is a matter of life or death. Your goal should be to be professional and ethical, and to just do the best you can.

Doing your best, of course, involves being prepared. Once I have gathered the facts and brainstormed various options and solutions, I write out what I am going to say so I can communicate it as calmly and succinctly as possible. Part of my script involves being honest about the fact that I feel terrible, as in: "I'm really upset I have to give you this bad news," or "I was up all night worrying about this." Humanizing the issue can soften the blow. And to this day, I practice. If I have a colleague with whom I can role play, I do that as well.

What if someone is asking for the impossible and won't take no for an answer? In these cases, you must be firm. Educate them as much as possible and give the reasons for your answer. No one likes to hear "no," so I try to avoid using that word. I love the phrase "What I can do is…" There is *always* something you can do, even if it is not exactly what the other person wants. Just offering to do *something* is better than nothing. If all else fails, maybe you offer to have your boss call the other person's boss to let them know the situation wasn't their fault. While they might not take you up on it, this action proves that you are willing to do what you can to help.

I also like to give people choices. Imagine you are stuck on an airplane due to a mechanical problem and the flight attendant says there will be a three hour delay. If the airline gives you a choice of getting off the plane or staying in your seat until the issue is fixed, the ball is in your court. While neither option is attractive, at least you feel like you have some control over the situation.

I try to find the silver lining in most situations, and if possible, turn the problem into a teaching moment. Unless the circumstance is highly confidential, I'll often ask someone junior to join me on a "bad news" call. I won't put the person on a speaker phone, but my colleague can still get a lot out of hearing my side of the conversation. Since they may have to make a call like this someday, what better way to learn than to hear me in a real-life situation? It's a win/win too, because having an audience helps me be my best, and after the call, I have someone with whom to debrief and commiserate!

Danielle also turns negative experiences into development opportunities by doing honest debriefs after a big project. She has everyone go around and say one thing another team member did well and one thing a team member could have done better. She finds these postmortems are the most effective way to crystalize lessons learned and ensure the insights are applied in the future.

In my experience, most people are reasonable. I've been in business a long time and I can count on one hand the times someone was totally irrational. If someone gets very angry and raises their voice, it is best for you to be as calm and soft-spoken as possible. And if someone is truly abusive, you should not allow the interaction to continue. Tell them you'll talk more about the issue when they can have a professional discussion, and disengage from the conversation.

PASS THE BATON, BREAK THROUGH THE GATE, AND CURE UNRESPONSIVENESS

I get asked all the time: "Karyn, how do I deal with the fact that I've been promoted but people are still reaching out to me instead of the new point of contact?" This is a terrific question! Step one is to make sure your subordinate has received the appropriate training and can, independently, answer most of the questions that will come their way. Step two is good communication. When introducing your subordinate, be clear they are now the main contact, as in: "Mary, of course I'm here for support, but Stephanie is going to be taking on the day-to-day interaction with you. I am confident that she will do a wonderful job." Step three is the most important and the hardest. When Mary reaches out to you instead of Stephanie, pretend you don't have the answer, as in: "I'm sorry Mary, but I'm not that close to this. Let me have Stephanie get back to you." After a couple of these conversations, Mary will realize she can get a quicker and better response from Stephanie.

Similarly, what if there is a gatekeeper who is holding you back from getting to the people with whom you need to interact? It is always better if you can bond with a gatekeeper and convince them your interests are aligned. Even better than just aligning your interests, if you can convince your gatekeeper that by opening the gate you can make them look good in front of their boss (or the person with whom you need to interact) that can be a huge win. However, sometimes there is a person who is threatened by you or your company and tries to block your progress. If this person is your day-to-day contact, it is very hard to go around or above them. If you do, it can have a devastating effect on your relationship. That's when you should bring in senior help.

There was once a gatekeeper at a major client of ours. Kate was a negative person who resisted engaging with us. She refused to introduce us to the people in other functions within her organization that could benefit from our solutions. My team tried many different approaches to no avail. If this happens to you, you might have to enlist the support of others in your organization to make individual contact at different levels.

In the case of Kate, that's exactly what my team did. Through independent networking, I had formed a relationship with a top executive at Kate's company. I contacted Jerry and suggested we meet for breakfast (of course) to catch up. I didn't go to the meeting with the intent to sell him anything, but I had done my homework so I knew a lot about his business issues. We talked about our families and some general business topics. I probed a bit on his business challenges and he opened up about some issues we were well suited to address.

When I casually mentioned our solutions, Jerry was surprised he hadn't heard about them. I was careful not to badmouth Kate the Gate, but when she found out about my breakfast, she was not happy. My account person simply said: "I'm so sorry, but I can't control what the CEO of my company does." As a courtesy, we invited Kate to the follow-up meeting with Jerry and another executive. Even though my team was frustrated with Kate, I asked them for something positive I could say about her in front of the executives. I insisted it be authentic and not a false compliment. We wanted to make her look good in the meeting. Kate was thrilled to get exposure with the executives, and had to admit at the end of the meeting our solutions would be helpful to the business. Kate has since become more of an advocate within her organization. Regardless, I've continued to maintain my direct contact with Jerry and was delighted when he introduced me to some other senior executives at his organization.

Many tough workplace situations are caused by unresponsive clients or co-workers whose lack of input is preventing you from doing your job. The best approach here involves communicating how they will benefit from getting back to you, and the consequences that will ensue if you don't get what you need. When all else fails, you MIGHT try this unique technique I learned from my friend Rich Isaac, founder and president of Sandler Training, Hauppauge, NY. Rich suggested sending an email with the subject line "Crocodiles." In the body of the message, you say: "After repeated attempts to connect with you, I haven't heard back, so I can only imagine one of three things happened:

1. You are crazy busy.
2. I've offended you in some way.
3. You've been eaten by crocodiles, in which case I need your address so I can send condolence flowers to your family.

Please let me know!"

This approach may be a little too far-fetched for most of us, but it will certainly get their attention!

I'M MAD AND I CAN'T TAKE IT ANYMORE

Let's turn the tables for a moment. What if you are the one with the grievance? Even if you are angry and completely in the right, it behooves you to be rational and professional. Everyone types irate emails, myself included. This is okay to do, but here's the important part—DON'T HIT SEND! You are bound to say something you'll later regret. IT systems claiming they can retrieve sent emails usually don't work when it really matters, so don't put yourself in that situation and stick the angry email in a draft folder. Wait until you calm down, and then re-read the message, checking the tone and thinking carefully about whether you really want to send it.

My husband always says he learned the right way to complain from me. I never complain just for the sake of it. If I'm going to the trouble, I do it with a purpose in mind. I also make sure I am talking with someone who has the authority to address my issue. For example, let's assume I've been given a hotel room next to the elevator and it is extremely noisy. I start by finding out who can make a room change, since I don't want to waste my time talking to the wrong person. I am clear on what I want, I'm firm but polite, and I don't lose my temper. If I have clout, I take advantage of this, and I let them know a potential consequence if I'm not accommodated, such as: "I am a frequent traveler. As you can see from my records, I stay at this hotel often and I have a lot of colleagues who do the same. I would hate to have to switch to the hotel across the street."

Sometimes I can't get what I want. In this example, perhaps the hotel is sold out. Then, I rethink my strategy and am very clear about communicating what I want instead. I might ask for a discount on the room rate. Or, I might want a note in my file saying I was dissatisfied and want to request a quieter room in the future.

I recently moved my elderly parents from Florida to an assisted living facility near my home in New York. Unfortunately, my mother was in the hospital for a week and my father wasn't coping well without her. The place is quite good, but there were a few serious mishaps the week my mother was away—of all times! As is the case with many elderly folks, my dad values his routine. His usual aide was out sick and the replacement showed up 90 minutes late, causing him to miss breakfast. The next day, he was not given his evening medications and after several phone calls, he had to pull the emergency cord to get attention.

I called the head of "Wellness" and politely explained it was important to avoid these situations, particularly when my mother was in the hospital. When something went awry a third time, I almost lost it. I decided it was time to call the big boss, but before doing so, wrote out my key talking points and rehearsed. On the call, I calmly introduced myself and offered a few compliments about what was going well (remember that sandwich way of giving feedback?). I then shared my concerns and frustrations using specific examples. I acknowledged there were many residents and I did not expect VIP treatment for my parents unless one was sick or in the hospital. The director listened, said all the right things, and assured me he would give extra attention to the matter and that similar incidents would not occur again. An additional benefit of the conversation? I've now developed a relationship with the director and I can reach out to him directly if there is an issue that warrants top level attention.

Words of Wisdom

"Your integrity is your biggest asset. Compromise on that and one day you will fail, and fail big."

—Simon Chadwick, chairman, Insights Association, and managing partner, Cambiar.

NEUTRALIZE TOXIC COWORKERS

I once had a peer who was not nice and didn't get along well with most of our co-workers. She often raised her voice and was demanding and demeaning in public forums. I struggled with how to deal with her. Others had tried talking to her about how her approach made them feel with no results. So, I decided to try something that was out of character for me. I walked in her office and closed the door loudly (just short of a slam). I said in a firm voice: "We are peers and need to set an example for working well together. I don't appreciate the way you speak to me. It's unacceptable and I need you to change it immediately." Then, I spun on my heel and walked out. Since this situation didn't involve a difference of opinion that needed to be talked through, I felt there was no point in engaging in a discussion. This altercation completely changed the way she interacted with me. While it's not my preferred approach, sometimes the best way to deal with a bully is to be tough back. I was strong and unwavering, and it worked.

Most of the time though, I prefer to address conflict more civilly. I once had a colleague who would whisper to the person next to him in meetings. I find this very frustrating, especially if I'm leading the meeting. Since I was an education major, the teacher in me wanted to call him out, but I opted to take the high road and address the issue behind closed doors. I kept my comments short and to the point: "Larry, I find it distracting when you engage in a private conversation during a group meeting. I value your contributions and would really appreciate it if you could either share your thoughts with everyone or wait until after the meeting to discuss them. Thanks so much." It worked, although now and again he did need a little reminder.

DID YOU KNOW?

If you frequently find yourself in tough spots at work as a result of mistakes, you might want to get more sleep! According to a survey commissioned by Glassdoor, nearly half (48 percent) of employed Americans are making blunders at work due to fatigue. Tiredness is a bigger distraction to workers than social media (19 percent) and personal communications (35 percent). And the mistakes we're talking about are not just typos. Twenty-four percent of the workers surveyed confessed to addressing a colleague or client by the wrong name or sending an ill-advised email due to low energy. Workers know it, too. They are so desperate to combat tiredness that 93 percent of respondents have taken action—with more cups of coffee as the most frequently cited remedy.

"SORRY, BUT..." IS NOT AN APOLOGY

I took up tennis as an adult and I'm addicted to it. Singles is harder physically, but it is less complex because it's just you against your opponent. If you mess up, you are only letting yourself down.

In contrast, doubles is much more of a team sport. You could make all your shots, but still be a terrible doubles player if you aren't watching out for your partner. A bad position or hitting the ball in the wrong place can put your partner in peril. I am grateful I've gotten better, but I still lack the confidence of someone who has played their whole life. I find it easy to say I'm sorry in tennis, because I still feel humbled by my lack of experience.

I like most of the people I play with, except Sally. Sally is a very good player, but whenever she misses, she makes an excuse: she couldn't see due to the glare of the building, she was having trouble with the shadows from the trees, the ball hit a soft spot on the court, and on and on. It's tiresome. We all miss—even the pros—so get over it!

Often, when you make a mistake, the first instinct is to blame someone else. According to Richard Bander and John Grinder, who developed an approach to communication called Neuro-linguistic Programming (NLP), some individuals live "at cause" while others live "at effect." Being "at cause" means we own and influence our own experiences, while being "at effect" means we give excuses and are mere passengers to our experiences.

Since it's more natural to live "at effect," we must push to be "at cause"—and this is especially relevant when a mistake occurs at work. Even if another department or person clearly made an error, try not to place blame. If you do it with an outside customer, you may think it makes you look better, but as a representative of your company, the blame game is unprofessional and doesn't reflect well on you. Rise above it and take responsibility. If the situation is an internal one and you point fingers, it is likely to come back to bite you. Instead of blaming, change the conversation from focusing on who caused the problem to how you're going to solve it.

You're human, and sometimes, you are just going to be wrong. You do your best and you try hard, but sometimes, you just mess up. No one likes to make a mistake, but when necessary, do the right thing and apologize. Take accountability and be genuine about it. "Sorry, but..." doesn't cut it. "I'm sorry I made a mistake with that status report, but the instructions were not clear" is not an apology, it is an excuse.

Words of Wisdom

"It's better to make a decision and be wrong, then not make a decision at all. Human nature rewards people who are decisive. The most successful people have all made mistakes."

—Seth Plattus, senior managing director and chief administrative officer at Cerberus Capital Management.

SURVEY SAYS: THE RISE OF INCIVILITY AT WORK

Christine Porath, an associate professor at Georgetown University's McDonough School of Business, has focused her career on incivility in the workplace. Incivility is defined as "the exchange of seemingly inconsequential inconsiderate words and deeds that violate conventional norms or workplace conduct." Sometimes it is blatant, like:

- Losing one's temper or yelling at someone in public.
- Rude or obnoxious behavior in the workplace.
- Badgering or backstabbing in the workplace.
- Withholding important customer/client information.
- Sabotaging a project or damaging someone's reputation.

And other times it may be a bit subtler, like:

- Arriving late to a meeting.
- Checking email or texting during a meeting.
- Not answering calls or responding to emails in a timely manner.
- Ignoring or interrupting a colleague in the workplace.
- Not saying "please" or "thank you."

In other words, many of the situations we define as difficult are the result of some degree of incivility. Porath discussed her research in a recent *New York Times* article. One survey of 4,500 doctors, nurses and other hospital personnel showed how incivility negatively impacts workplace focus. Seventy-one percent of respondents tied disruptive behavior, such as abusive, condescending or insulting personal conduct, to medical errors, and 27 percent tied such behavior to patient deaths.

A second Porath study with Amir Erez, a management professor at the University of Florida, demonstrated people working in an environment characterized by incivility miss information that is right in front of them. In the research, the experimenter belittled the peer group of the participants, who then performed 33 percent worse on anagram word puzzles and came up with 39 percent fewer creative ideas during a brainstorming task.

Porath and Erez followed up this study with another in which a stranger—a "busy professor" encountered en route to the experiment—was rude to participants. Their performance was 61 percent worse on word puzzles, and they produced 58 percent fewer ideas in the brainstorming task than those who had not been treated rudely. Intriguingly, the researchers found the same pattern for those who merely witnessed incivility: they performed 22 percent worse on word puzzles and produced 28 percent fewer ideas in the brainstorm.

No one likes incivility, of course, but Porath measured steep workplace costs through a poll of 800 managers and employees in 17 industries that was published in *Harvard Business Review.* According to the results, of workers who have been on the receiving end of incivility:

- 48 percent intentionally decreased their work effort.
- 47 percent intentionally decreased the time spent at work.
- 38 percent intentionally decreased the quality of their work.
- 80 percent lost work time worrying about the incident.
- 63 percent lost work time avoiding the offender.
- 66 percent said their performance declined.
- 78 percent said their commitment to the organization declined.
- 12 percent said they left their job because of the uncivil treatment.
- 25 percent admitted to taking their frustration out on customers.

HR professionals too have reported just one incident of incivility can soak up weeks of attention and effort. Per a study conducted by Accountemps and reported in *Fortune,* managers and executives at Fortune 1000 firms spend 13 percent of their work time—or seven weeks a year—dealing with the aftermath of incivility.

How can we as individuals reduce the incidence of incivility? The first step is to honestly examine your own behavior and how you interact with others, and if you think there's room for improvement, seek coaching. Model respect, common courtesy, listening, and tolerance for ideas different from your own. Assume people are good unless proven otherwise, refraining from jumping to negative conclusions about the motives of others. When in an altercation, try to see the situation from the other person's point of view, look for common ground, and be forgiving—because everyone makes mistakes!

TYPES OF DIFFICULT PERSONALITIES

Alexandra Levit had these ideas for working with a variety of challenging colleagues.

Sam the Slacker: The slacker is not a fan of work and will do anything to avoid taking on new responsibilities. He seldom meets deadlines without being prodded and takes advantage of those who offer help. If you're dealing with a Sam, don't enable this behavior. Interact with him as little as possible so you don't get recruited into taking on additional work.

Izzy the Incompetent: Izzy may be a perfectly nice person who wants to do a good job, but for whatever reason, she's just not right for her position. If you find yourself in the situation of having to babysit her, resist the urge to take over. Assess what parts of a task she's good at already, and what parts you think she's able to learn. Even as a colleague, you can suggest certain training that will help her acquire necessary skills.

Freddie the Fraud: The fraud takes credit for other people's accomplishments while exaggerating his own. If you and Freddie have the same boss, keep a careful eye on him and make sure your manager knows what you're doing at all times so Freddie doesn't swoop in and hijack your image as the competent and hardworking one.

Bill the Backstabber: Bill wants that juicy project or promotion and he'll stop at nothing to get it. He knows how to manipulate people so he looks like the favorite and will step on anyone who interferes with his goals. Cope with Bill by accepting he'll never be a gracious team player. You'll be more likely to gain his cooperation if you make clear what's in it for him.

Violet the Vague: Violet expects you to be a mind-reader. She doesn't believe in sharing information proactively or giving specific direction, so working with her involves a lot of guesswork. Master your interactions with Violet by automatically assuming responsibilities and then asking her lots of questions. Seek help completing new tasks from other colleagues and then show Violet your work so she has something to react to.

Maria the Micromanager: She's the opposite of Violet, dictating exactly how to do the work and watching over every step in the process without allowing you to make any decisions or take any actions independently. Improve your relationship with Maria by offering her examples where you felt you could have worked more effectively if you weren't on such a short leash. Suggest ways to keep her in the loop, such as weekly reports or weekly meetings, so she doesn't feel she needs to check in as much.

Barry the Bully: This person doesn't think you can do anything right. Deal with him by swallowing your apprehension, putting on your armor, and walking into his office with a controlled and reasonable tone. Get what you need and get out, avoiding public altercations or gossiping about him with your co-workers. Both reactions will reflect poorly on you.

CHAPTER SUMMARY

- Whenever dealing with a conflict or a negative interaction, keep in mind most people won't remember the issue, but they *will* remember how it was handled. In fact, a favorable outcome could result in a closer relationship.
- All difficult situations have a beginning, middle and end. From the minute the problem is identified, ensure you get through these phases as quickly and professionally as possible, keeping the issue contained and not letting it blow out of proportion.
- When someone is angry or frustrated, they often won't be able to hear what you have to say until they can get their points off their chest. They need to "empty their glass of water." The best thing you can do in this situation is listen.
- No one likes to hear "no," so try to avoid that word. Instead, use the effective phrase: "What I can do is…" There is *always* something you can do, even if it is not exactly what the other person wants. Just offering to do *something* is better than nothing.
- Even if you are completely in the right, it behooves you to be rational and professional. It's okay to write an irate email, as long as you don't send it right away. In the heat of anger, you are bound to say something you'll later regret.
- Often, when you make a mistake, the first instinct is to blame someone else. This does not reflect well on you. Instead, rise above it and take responsibility. Remember, "sorry, but…" is not a genuine apology.

CHAPTER SIX

SKILLING UP: LEARNING WHAT YOU NEED TO SUCCEED

Building relationships and looking the part will get you pretty far in business, but ultimately you need to deliver the goods. In other words, you have to master the skills to do your job—especially if you want to move up. Every position, company, and industry will have different day-to-day job skills, but there are some universal ones such as financial acumen, negotiation, sales, public speaking, business writing, client service, and time management that are critical to succeeding in just about any business.

My father and all of his friends were business owners. Milton had a discount clothing store in Staten Island, Abe owned a gas station in Brooklyn, and my father owned a sewing machine and vacuum cleaner store on 85th Street and Amsterdam Avenue in Manhattan. They were self-employed and relied on their own smarts to run their businesses. I like to think of them as the entrepreneurs of their generation.

Our store was named Active Sewing Machine Company. The name "Active" was chosen carefully. Before Google, if you wanted to find a retail establishment, you went to the Yellow Pages where things were listed in alphabetical order by category. Since Active was at the top of the alphabet, when a potential customer searched under Sewing Machines or Vacuum Cleaners, they saw Active before going any further down the list. It was the 1950's version of search optimization!

I learned a lot about business from my father. For example, when I was young, I didn't understand the difference between revenue and profits. I couldn't comprehend why my father would rather sell a used Electrolux for $125 versus a brand new one for $300. Three hundred dollars was certainly a lot more money than $125, wasn't it? My father explained he would buy old, used, or broken machines for a nominal fee and then repair them, paint them, and sell them as remodeled, thus keeping the majority of the money as profit. On the other hand, when he bought a new machine from the manufacturer, he had to pay the manufacturer almost as much as he sold the machine for, yielding a very small margin (this is the difference between a product or service's selling price and its cost of production). Therefore, the used machine was a much more lucrative deal.

This story taught me a lot about return on investment (**ROI** = (Net Profit / Cost of Investment) x 100). However, in my first role as a general manager, I still felt unprepared for reading a balance sheet (a statement of the assets, liabilities, and capital of a company at a particular point in time) or a P&L (a profit and loss statement that recaps a company's expenses).

As we'll talk about in Chapter Nine, it's important to take initiative in managing your own career. Because I didn't have formal finance education, and this was a potential blind spot for me, I was assertive in asking for help and training in finance.

When I was invited to be part of a formal mentoring program, I requested the CFO as my mentor. I also asked if I could take an American Management Association course called *Finance for the Non-Financial Manager*. It provided a great set of basic skills for understanding how to read and interpret financial reports. Today, there are more options than ever, and many are online and/or free. From the comfort of your home, you can quickly master a variety of business finance skills from academic institutions like Harvard, UPenn, and MIT, as well as online course repositories Coursera, Udemy, and EdX.

Words of Wisdom

> *"Work as hard as you can, make the most of every opportunity, and push yourself to learn all while being authentically you. It will set you apart, fuel your career growth, and make you irreplaceable."*
>
> *—Ariann Langsam, director, Pilot Corporation of America.*

NEGOTIATING YOUR VALUE

My favorite business story from my father has to do with a man and some screws. One day, a man came into the store looking for an obsolete set of screws for his sewing machine. He had been searching for them all over and no one seemed to have what he needed. My father said: "I think I might have just what you are looking for," and went up to the store's attic. After searching for 10 minutes, my father found the exact screws. He came back down with a big smile: "You're in luck!" he said. "I had a feeling that I had them. That will be one dollar, please."

"One dollar?!" the man exclaimed. "One dollar for four screws. What are you, crazy?" Without hesitation, my father tossed the screws behind the counter and calmly said: "I'm so sorry; I don't seem to have them."

This story has stayed with me as a great example of valuing your product or service. When you provide something that meets a need of your client or customer, you cannot be afraid to charge for the value you are providing. A friend of mine is an author and speaker and has experienced increased demand for her services. She hadn't raised her speaking fee in years and was nervous to do it. I suggested she give it a try, explaining she could always go back to her lower price if clients resisted. She raised the fee, and guess what? No one even blinked!

In my business, clients will sometimes ask for a freebie. They might say since the information they want is "just sitting there," it wouldn't be that much work for us to simply to give it to them.

One of my co-workers had a great answer for this. He said he tells clients he was nearly arrested outside his local supermarket. When the surprised client asks why, he says he got caught taking a soup can out of the store. Since it was "just sitting there," he thought, why not just take it? This certainly makes the point that value goes beyond the product's availability.

Understanding the value of your product or service is critical when faced with a negotiation. There are many tips regarding negotiations, but I tend to focus on these:

1. Have pride in your products and services and know the value they bring to your customers.
2. Know at what point you are willing to walk away.
3. Weigh the potential damage to the long-term relationship

if there isn't some level of win-win. The win-win doesn't need to be equal, but both parties need to get something from the negotiation.

Growing up in my family, negotiation was a varsity sport. My parents were from the Depression generation, and their mantra was: "Never pay retail." For example, when my parents moved to Florida and bought a condominium, they decorated it beautifully. When we went to see it and complimented them on the stunning couch, my parents enthusiastically told us about the "deal." "We went to Store L and saw the couch," my mother began. "But then we went over to store M and saw the same couch for 10 percent less," my father chimed in. "So we went back to Store L, and they not only matched the price, but they took an extra $50 off, so we bought it from Store L," they finished with big smiles on their faces.

Having been raised this way, I enjoy the art of negotiation. When I was in Shanghai, a group of young women from my office took me to a shopping area where negotiation is expected. The shopkeepers are real pros at this. Most Americans can't help but remember they are quibbling over pennies, so they give in quickly, but I took this as a challenge and impressed my Asian employees with my negotiation skills.

In order to teach Danielle to negotiate, I took her to Canal Street in New York City, where it is common to haggle on price. It can be a very uncomfortable thing if you've never done it, but just as with networking and interviewing, practice helps. Danielle was shocked when we walked out of one shop over $1 on a barrette she wanted. But, we were keeping in mind Tip #2: Be willing to walk away.

Of course, life being what it is, walking away is not always possible. I came face-to-face with this situation when I had to go to a major retailer to negotiate an important contract. Before I left for the meeting my boss said: "Karyn, don't come back without a deal!" Ugh! That was the worst thing he could have said, since it meant I had to make the deal no matter what. So, I tapped into some other negotiation strategies. I used multi-year and quantity discounts to help get to their budget. I remembered to "get when you have to give," so when they asked for leeway on the T&Cs (terms and conditions), I asked for something in return, such as a referral or the ability to use their name with other prospects.

Recalling Tip #3, I'm also careful about when to give in on a short-term issue in service of the long-term relationship. One of my best client relationships started because I didn't charge what I could have. I was in California on business, and as is my custom, I got up really early to go to the hotel gym. I stopped in the little coffee bar to get my fix, and there was a gentleman there with whom I exchanged pleasantries. There were two little tables next to each other in the shop, so I decided to be friendly and continue the conversation by joining him.

To my surprise, it turned out this man was the new CEO of a key customer of ours, and he was in town for an important board meeting. Due to a major enhancement to our service, my company planned to increase prices within the next month. The CEO was happy we had met so serendipitously because he was concerned about the price increase and wanted to talk with someone at my company about it.

He approached the conversation in exactly the right way. He didn't deny the value of the enhancement, or the appropriateness of the price increase. Instead, he took me into his confidence and explained the challenges he was facing. He explained he was hired to turnaround the company and would be forced to lay off staff. The price increase might mean additional layoffs, since he had profit targets he needed to deliver. He humbly asked me if I would be willing to defer the increase until he got his shop in order. I weighed the pros and cons in my mind and quickly agreed. It was a risk, but it paid off. This CEO has become not only a valued client but a friend. He has generously given his time, speaking at company events for me and being an advocate for our services. I made the right call in balancing the short-term benefit of the added revenue versus the long-term benefit of the deeper relationship.

ENLISTING YOUR TROOPS

When I first started working, we would send a client a contract, and they would quickly sign it and send it back. Today, our clients employ scores of lawyers and procurement personnel, and we have to respond with a staff of professionals on our side as well. It has gotten much more complicated. If you are faced with a situation where you are negotiating with Procurement or Legal and you aren't a seasoned negotiator, I suggest you get someone with more experience to assist you if possible. You will be at a disadvantage dealing with a pro who does this for a living. It would be like me playing tennis singles against Serena Williams.

In the meantime, whenever you get a chance to negotiate, view it as good practice! For instance, the next time you check into a hotel, ask innocently for an upgrade. If the place isn't sold out, the attendant might give you a nicer room to entice you to become a loyal customer. You'll hone your skills AND get a little extra comfort during your stay!

Words of Wisdom

"Everyone has their own style, intellect, goals, and areas of expertise. Develop them, nurture them, focus on them, own them, but never stop listening and learning."

—Stephanie Dismore, vice president and general manager, HP.

SALES SKILLS FOR NON-SALESPEOPLE

Good sales skills are essential even if you have no intention of ever being an official salesperson. Anytime you are trying to influence another person to get something you want, you are selling. Sales techniques and strategies have changed a lot over the years. In my early days of selling, my success was primarily based on tenacity, responsiveness, and the ability to build relationships. I would push myself to see as many clients as possible, generate as many proposals as possible, and get back to people as quickly as possible—even if it meant working late. What better time to convince a prospect you will go above and beyond for them than when you are trying to get their business?

I'll never forget the time a major telecommunications company asked my company to bid on a huge project. While people often complain about competition, I say it's a gift. Competition makes you better. It forces you to be smarter, faster, and more creative. In this case, the client wanted 24 different cost options. This was ridiculous, of course, but I had to do what they asked. I remember it well, because it was Thanksgiving weekend and I was pregnant with Danielle. We were at my parents' house for the holiday, and I locked myself away in my childhood bedroom working on the proposal at my little white schoolgirl desk.

The story has a happy ending. The client was impressed all 24 options were well thought out. Even though my company wasn't the lowest price option, I won the business and earned a contract worth over a million dollars.

While hard work and responsiveness worked well in this case, my approach to selling was not as strategic as it could have been. In Chapter Four, I talked about the sales tape program that helped me acquire new skills. When listening to one of the tapes, I heard something that shocked me. The speaker said a good salesperson should only talk 10 percent of the time in a sales meeting with a new prospect. Ten percent! I rewound the tape and listened again to be sure I heard it right.

This was not exactly how I was handling my sales meetings. I usually went into a meeting with my sales deck and talked through, slide by slide, A through Z. I covered the company background, how long we were in business, our products, our methodology, our benefits, etc. I only came up for air when the prospect had a question.

The trainer on the tape explained that instead just talking at the prospect, you should engage them in a dialogue, asking questions and uncovering unmet needs. This was interesting, but would it really work? I wanted to give it a try.

At my next sales team meeting, I explained the concept and asked what people thought. My team members were all as skeptical as I was, but Mary said she wanted to give it a try, too. She had an upcoming meeting with a prospect at a baked goods company nearby, and we decided to go together. Mary had met the prospect once before and was concerned because Sharon was quiet. Would this new method work with an introvert, we wondered?

We had our slide deck as backup, but we didn't take it out. We were very relaxed and laid back in the meeting, asking questions about Sharon's business and probing for more detail. We were active listeners, nodding and smiling. For her part, Sharon was fully engaged and even animated. She shared information with us we would not have gotten if we were busy pitching the whole time. While we never covered most of what was in our slides, it didn't matter. Instead, we covered the things that were relevant to the client, and those were the things she remembered. Less than a week later, Sharon requested a proposal.

It's amazing how easy and effective it is to just let people talk. One time, my boss and I met with the executive team from an entertainment company in Los Angeles. When we arrived, the CEO asked us to stop in his private office before joining his team in the conference room. With slicked back black hair, a black pinstriped suit and gold jewelry, he looked like something out of a *Godfather* movie. He led us into his palatial office, where we sat on his couch talking—or should I say listening. The guy talked nonstop for 20 minutes. When we met up with the other members of his team in the conference room, Dapper Dan put his arms around us and said to his staff: "I really like these folks. I like what they have to say!"

The art of sales continues to evolve and is going through another transformation right now. It was once revolutionary to go from the "pitch" to "strategic selling," in which you ask questions to uncover business issues and opportunities like Mary and I did with Sharon. While strategic selling is still an effective method, the best salespeople today go beyond it. They go into meetings already knowing a lot about the company and its needs. They still let the prospect do most of the talking, but they are ready with a variety of solutions, often tapping into expertise from technical or product specialists to support the details.

Another sales technique that has served me well is "don't sell after the close"—otherwise known as "know when to stop talking." Allow me to illustrate. When Danielle was three-years -old, she met her best friend, Rachel. They were inseparable, so it was no surprise they always wanted their playdates to last longer and there were frequent pleas for sleepovers, to which Rachel's mom and I were usually happy to oblige—despite the fact we lived 30 minutes apart.

One day, when the girls were about six-years-old, the usual begging began: "Pleeeeease," they cried. This time, instead of merely giving in, I asked them to put together a presentation on why they should be granted a sleepover. It had already been a long day, so they needed to make it good and address our objections.

The two girls ran upstairs to work on their proposal. They used poster board, construction paper, glue, crayons, and markers. Upon their return to the kitchen, they took turns presenting their case, using their illustrations for support. They were adorable—and compelling! Before they could even get to the end, we conceded.

When they kept going, wanting to say more, I put up my hand and said: "Stop! You've already convinced us. Don't say anything more that might change our minds." In other words, don't sell after the close. Danielle remembers that moment and uses it in her business dealings today.

DID YOU KNOW?

There is a famous story about a boilermaker who was hired to fix a huge steamship boiler system that was not working well.

After listening to the engineer's description of the problems and asking a few questions, he went to the boiler room. He looked at the maze of twisting pipes, listened to the thump of the boiler and the hiss of the escaping steam for a few minutes, and felt some pipes with his hands. Then he hummed softly to himself, reached into his overalls and took out a small hammer, and tapped a bright red valve one time. Immediately, the entire system began working perfectly, and the boilermaker went home.

When the steamship owner received a bill for $1,000.00, he became outraged and complained that the boilermaker had only been in the engine room for 15 minutes. He requested an itemized bill, so the boilermaker sent him a bill that read as follows:

For tapping the valve:	$.50
For knowing where to tap:	$999.50
TOTAL:	$1,000.00

On his website, digital expert Jeffa Cubed used this story as an example of how know-how is more important than a title. You can have a hundred titles, but you *must* be able to apply what you know. Education will help you to find a job, while education combined with insight and creativity will define your future.

Lots of folks can and do "tap the valve"—very few know precisely *where* to tap and *why*. Be *that* tapper.

PRESENTING WITH FINESSE

My mother is an extrovert. My mother's sister was an extrovert. In fact, that whole side of my family is extroverted. When we'd get together, you could hardly hear anyone talk because it was so loud. If we went to a wedding or a big party, we'd all be out on the dance floor forming a conga line, embarrassing our family members who didn't share our lack of inhibition. Given my outgoing personality, presenting in front of an audience is something I relish. But I realize not everyone feels this way and presenting can be intimidating. Even as a seasoned professional, I have had my share of difficult presenting moments. The good news is the ability to effectively speak in public can be learned and improved with some training and practice.

While I had given many slide presentations to small and medium-sized groups, the first time I had to speak with a microphone in a large auditorium, a strange thing happened. I expected I might experience the usual butterflies, but as I walked up to the microphone, my heart started pounding like it was going to burst out of my chest! Nothing like this had ever happened to me before, and at first I thought I was having a heart attack. After I started speaking, I settled down and thankfully didn't have to be rushed to the emergency room, but it definitely shook me up.

I've since come up with a few strategies to avoid this kind of near-panic. I get to the venue early and, when feasible, stand up on the stage or do a dress rehearsal where I will be presenting. This helps me acclimate to the surroundings. I always make sure I have my first couple of sentences down pat so I get off to a good start, and I try to remember to breathe. Finally, I make sure I am dressed in something that makes me feel fabulous and confident.

My son Eric added black is always a safe color to wear, and certain patterns (like small plaid or gingham) don't look their best on video. And, don't wear jewelry that might jiggle or be distracting.

I also make sure to find a "friendly" in the audience. In my experience, there is usually at least one person who is actively listening to the presentation. They are engaged, often nodding and sometimes smiling, but clearly paying attention to what I'm saying. It is a best practice to make eye contact with individual audience members and hold it for a second or two before scanning for another person with whom to connect. When I find one of these "friendlies," I draw inspiration and support from them and look at them often as I speak.

If by chance you lose your place or make a mistake while presenting, just go on. Don't stop or apologize. The audience probably won't notice a small flub, but they will notice something you draw major attention to. Also, at some point you may be faced with a situation in which there is a technical problem and your slides or materials are not available. If you know your subject, you should still be able to get across the main points of your presentation. Do the best you can, and you are sure to impress your audience if you keep your cool.

When I started playing tennis and was nervous, I would sometimes get "into my head," which would distract me and cause me to start making mistakes. I heard about a book that made a huge difference in my tennis game, called *The Inner Game of Tennis: The Classic Guide to the Mental Side of Peak Performance* by W. Timothy Gallwey. There are many good tips in it, but here's one that can be effectively used in public speaking. The author outlined the concept of role playing to help develop confidence.

He'll introduce the idea to a student by saying something like: "Imagine I'm the director of a TV series. Knowing you are an actor who plays tennis, I ask if you would do a bit part as a top-flight tennis player. Don't worry about how you hit the ball, just adopt professional mannerisms and swing the racket with supreme self-assurance. Above all, your face must express no self-doubt. Really get into the role." Gallwey said in doing this exercise, he observed remarkable changes in the person's game as they embodied the role. So, if you are nervous presenting, pretend you are playing the part of a famous newscaster or TV talk show host. Fake it until you make it!

On the subject of confidence, my friend Wendy shared a story about her experience growing up with a father who was an actor. She and her four siblings would sit at the dinner table and their father would bellow to one of them, "Stand up! Give me five minutes on ketchup!"

Wendy replied: "Well, ketchup is red and it is made of tomatoes and—"

"Buzz!" he'd yell. "Sit down, that was terrible. Mike, stand up and give me five minutes on rocks!" And on it would go.

Wendy told me she'd never know exactly what was coming and their dad wasn't one to worry about hurting their feelings or being politically correct. The kids hated this exercise at the time, but years later, they recognize it gave them the ability to walk into a room and speak confidently to anyone about anything. Wendy's TV producer sister even won an Emmy because she was able to talk her way onto an award-winning children's show. If you want to improve your extemporaneous speaking skills, you might try this exercise too!

And that's the thing. No matter how good you are, you can always hone your presentation skills. I once took an intensive training class during which I was videotaped. The process was uncomfortable, but effective. While watching back my video, I realized I made this annoying clicking sound with my tongue when I presented. Ouch! Fortunately, by just being aware I was doing it, I was able to rid myself of that habit.

As I've said, I'm a big fan of practice presentations. The more feedback you can get, the better you will be. For example, when preparing for a big speech to an industry association, I invited a woman from my company's Learning and Development team to watch my practice presentation and provide critical feedback. I knew the other people watching would give feedback on my content and slides, but not on my presentation style or mannerisms. She gave me two helpful comments. One, my hair kept falling into my face and it was distracting when I repeatedly pushed it out of the way, and two, I had a tendency to stand with one knee bent. To this day, I always use a little extra hairspray when I know I am going to be presenting, and I try my best to stand up straight.

While practice is important, you don't want to overdo it either. If you memorize every word or read your presentation, you may sound stiff. Try to find a few places where you can ad lib a little.

Sometimes, you can get help with presentations in unexpected places. My son Eric did an internship at my company the summer before his senior year of college, and since we have different last names, he preferred not to make a big deal out of being my son. I was giving an internal webinar on our annual client satisfaction results, and since Eric had been the captain of both the extemporaneous speaking and the debate clubs in high school, I asked him to come to my practice presentation. He had some useful advice, including tips on voice modulation and a suggestion I talk to the coming slide before switching to it in order to encourage anticipation of my next remarks. During the live presentation, Eric was beaming. Afterwards, he turned to his fellow interns and said proudly: "How cool that my mom just used my feedback in her presentation to the whole company!" To which they replied: "What? Karyn is your mom?" Oops. He blew his own cover!

Regardless of what you are presenting, I recommend a variation of the "Tell, Do, Tell" strategy I shared earlier. In the "Tell, Show, Tell" method, you tell them upfront what you will be presenting, then show them your content, and finally, tell them the key points they should take away. Remember, most people can't remember more than three to five key concepts, so be succinct. In my business, we often present data. I support the "What, So What, and Now What" approach here. Most people stop at the "What," or the facts. You will have a much more compelling talk if you also discuss the "So What," or what the facts mean, and finally, the "Now What?" or the actions the audience should take as a result. As an example, here's how I used this format when presenting my company's client satisfaction results.

- What? Clients are satisfied with Product A and Product B, but there are very few clients using Product B. The awareness rate for Product B is substantially lower than Product A.
- So What? Low awareness of Product B is causing poor sales.
- Now What? We need to launch an external marketing campaign and internal education program to increase awareness of Product B.

COMMON PUBLIC SPEAKING MISTAKES

- *Talking loudly and enthusiastically.* People think this is better than talking in a low, monotone voice, and it generally is. But it's more important to modulate. Even an upbeat voice over an extended period can get irritating.
- *Over or under gesturing.* Your hands and gestures should be like punctuation to make a point.
- *Standing awkwardly on stage.* Some people are good at moving around on the stage, so for them, walking around works. If you aren't a walker, it is best to use a podium.
- *Having too many words on your slides.* It is better not to have a lot of words on the slides in the first place. More slides don't cost more money. However, when presenting to a global audience, your remarks will be easier for people to follow if there are words to read along as you speak.
- *Saying different words than are on your slides.* If you have to have words, first read what is on the slide and then ad lib additional points. Otherwise, it's hard for the audience to know if they should be listening to you or reading the slide.
- *Confusing a presentation with a handout.* Very often the slides are too dense, because they are also being used as a handout or leave-behind. If you need both, make two decks.
- *Not pausing.* One of the most effective ways to make a point is to be quiet. While in front of a group, a moment of silence can feel like forever, so count to five silently.
- *Going over on time.* This is rude, especially if there are other presenters. Time your presentation during your practice sessions and cut if needed. Do not shorten the time by talking faster!

BUSINESS WRITING SAVVY

Just as you need to dress to impress, you need to write to impress as well. It's important to keep your audience in mind and communicate with an appropriate level of formality. Your style should also differ depending on whether the communication is text, email, handwritten, or in a more formal document. Regardless, don't get tripped up by spelling errors or commonly misused words. My personal pet peeves are "then" versus "than" and using "I" when it should be "me," but there are so many more! Fortunately, there are just as many online resources to help as there are errors.

Blaise Pascal, the French mathematician, logician, physicist, and theologian, said: "I'm sorry I wrote you such a long letter; I didn't have time to write a short one." While this may seem counter-intuitive, it's true. Writing something short and to the point often takes much longer since it requires constant evaluation of what's most important and what can be left out. Just because you did the research and have pages of documentation doesn't mean you need to use it all. If you feel you must include the supporting information, consider putting it in an Appendix so your recipient can choose to read the extra depth or not.

For business correspondence, I prefer simple, clear language and bullet points versus long verbiage. I try to avoid jargon and the dreaded acronym, especially those not universally understood. While I do think there is a place for the occasional smiley face or "LOL," remember to stay professional and don't get too cutesy. While not appropriate for all communication, I often like to put an executive summary upfront and close with next steps. Finally, if the document I am writing is very important, I will often have a colleague review it. It takes an extra step but results in a better deliverable.

One final point: considering today's technology, you must assume anything sent in email has the potential to be passed on. If you've written something you aren't comfortable having everyone see (such as a tough feedback), have an in-person conversation instead.

Words of Wisdom

"My one piece of advice, which I think is especially relevant in today's age of texting, short-hand, and increasingly casual work environments: always err on the side of professionalism in your written and verbal communications. Also, be thoughtful in the way you carry yourself as it is never too early to begin honing your executive presence."

—Diana Schildhouse, senior vice president, Mattel.

CLIENT SERVICE EXCELLENCE

Understanding how to deliver great client service is a necessary skill whether your "client" is an external customer or someone inside your organization. Since Danielle works as a client lead for a major piece of business, I asked her to share some of her best advice on client service excellence and she was happy to oblige.

When asked to define what good client service means, Danielle said "I think it's easier to start with what it's not. It's not saying yes to everything, or believing the client is always right. Client service is not sacrificing employee satisfaction for the client's every whim," she said.

"First and foremost, like other relationships, client ones are based on empathy. At the end of the day, the role of a client services lead is to advocate and be the voice of their client internally and do the same for their company with the client." Here are some other dos and don'ts to develop your client service skills:

- DO devote your full attention to clients while in meetings, meaning everyone is an active participant and no one is multi-tasking on their phone or computer.
- DON'T talk to clients about other business on which you work. They want to feel like you're focusing on their needs.
- DO communicate with team members before bringing them into a client conversation to ensure they have the appropriate context.
- DON'T haphazardly add people into client email chains, and when you do copy people in, make sure they know why they are being included. Is this just FYI, are you asking them to take action, or do you want their opinion?
- DON'T put too much information in automatic "Out of Office" email messages. A single contact filling in for you is usually sufficient.
- DO respond to all client emails as soon as possible, even if just to confirm receipt and indicate you'll get back to them with a more thorough response.
- DON'T lose touch with your client after you deliver a project. Ask how they are using your deliverables and what new business issues have come up.
- DO look for additional opportunities to grow the relationship: take advantage of opportunities to attend internal client meetings, trainings, and focus groups.

- DON'T keep it in your head. Document client interactions in a program like Evernote or Salesforce and share your notes with other team members.
- DO be honest. If you don't have the expertise or bandwidth to serve the client to your usual standard say so.

Besides excelling in your job, strong client relationships have numerous benefits. Of course, there are sales implications. When a client likes you, it's much easier to upsell a new offering than when the person is indifferent. A happy client will also introduce you to people in their organization and make referrals within the industry.

Also, when you are friendly with a client, every day is more satisfying. You can anticipate their needs and you know how they like things, so projects run smoothly. Clients who have your back may give you suggestions for improving your product or service, tip you off to competitive threats, or alert you in advance if there's a potential problem with the business looming. And as mutual trust builds over time, there's less stress all around, and it is simply more fun!

TIME MANAGEMENT

There is a great YouTube video by director Steve Pemberton from the UK that goes something like this:

I decide to wash the car; I start toward the garage and notice the mail on the table. Okay, I'm going to wash the car, but first I'm going to go through the mail. I lay the car keys down on the desk, discard the junk mail and I notice the trash can is full. Okay, I'll just put the bills on my desk and take the trash can out, but since I'm going to be near the mailbox anyway, I'll pay these few bills first. Oh, there's the coke I was drinking. I need to put my coke further away from the computer, or maybe I'll pop it into the fridge to keep it cold for a while. I head towards the kitchen and my flowers catch my eye; they need some water. I set the coke on the counter and ooh, oh! Someone left the TV remote in the kitchen. We will never think to look in the kitchen tonight when we want to watch television so I'd better put it back where it belongs. I splash some water into the pots and onto the floor. I throw the remote onto the sofa and I head down the hall trying to figure out what it was I was going to do.

END OF DAY: The car isn't washed, the bills are unpaid, the coke is sitting on the kitchen counter, the flowers are half watered, and I can't seem to find my car keys! When I try to figure out how come nothing got done today, I'm baffled because I KNOW I WAS BUSY ALL DAY LONG!

This is exactly how it sometimes feels in the office. You start on one task and ping, you get an email that leads you in another direction and then someone swings by and asks you a question, and so on. While we all have days like this, in general you want to keep this tendency in check.

It helps to know yourself and find a method that fits your style. I'm a morning person, so I block time in the morning for more difficult tasks that require me to be at my best. I'm not as alert by late afternoon, and I'm worthless late at night. In fact, I have a "no talking" after 10 p.m. rule so my husband doesn't try to engage me in a serious conversation when I'm at my worst. I'm also much more productive if I've gotten enough sleep and if I've had time to work out. I never miss a meal, so that isn't an issue for me, but I've seen colleagues get really irritable and unproductive when they haven't eaten (my kids call this hangry).

In terms of time management and general organization, I find lists work really well. I get a lot of satisfaction from crossing things off, and the list keeps me focused. Sometimes if I'm feeling overwhelmed, just writing everything down and getting it all out of my head helps. I have a few different kinds of lists, including a daily to-do list, a long-term list, and more specific lists organized by projects and people.

I like to get into the office early so I have some quiet time. I start each day by looking at my calendar and going through my daily to-do list. I don't go crazy with prioritization, but I do identify which items must get done today, and those are the ones I make sure I focus on completing. The others can move on to tomorrow.

If time management is tough for you, here are some additional strategies to consider:

- Turn off the sound on your computer and don't let incoming emails distract you unless they are urgent. Take advantage of technology. For example, search functions in email programs are now so advanced there's no need to spend lots of time categorizing and filing.
- Start and end meetings on time, or even end early. Since there is nothing magical about 60 minutes, I changed our calendar scheduler to make the default 50 minutes! Build in time in between meetings to check messages and/or take a bio break.
- Block time to work on an important project! It takes discipline to do this, but it is the only way you can get bigger things done with higher quality. Say no to non-important and non-urgent tasks so you can protect this time.

SURVEY SAYS: SALARY NEGOTIATION AND FOLLOW-UP SALES SKILLS FOUND WANTING

According to one recent Payscale initiative that involved 31,000 U.S. professionals, less than half of respondents have ever asked for a raise in their current field. For the 57 percent who have not asked, the reasons most often cited are: my employer gave me a raise before I needed to ask for one (38 percent), I'm uncomfortable negotiating salary (28 percent), and I didn't want to be perceived as pushy (19 percent).

Payscale found, compared with men, women are more uncomfortable with negotiation. Women said their uneasiness with this process is the reason they didn't negotiate 31 percent of the time, whereas men only referenced the same reasoning 23 percent of the time. This isn't a surprise to Linda Babcock, an economics professor, the co-founder of Carnegie Mellon University's Negotiation Academy, and the author of *Women Don't Ask* and *Ask For It*. In her research, Babcock found, when asked to choose a metaphor to describe the negotiation process, women picked "going to the dentist." For comparison, men chose "winning a ballgame."

In Babcock's research, men were shown to initiate negotiations about four times as often as women. Twenty percent of adult women never negotiate at all, even when it may be appropriate, and women enter negotiations with pessimistic expectations about what wage increases are available. Thus, if they do negotiate, they don't ask for much: a full 30 percent less than men!

Interestingly, the Payscale research illustrated women aren't the only group that could improve on the negotiation front. Millennials are also less likely to negotiate salary than other generations, at least when it comes to solidifying their first professional position. Sixty percent of millennials don't negotiate salary when receiving their first job offers. Payscale offered this is an extremely costly career decision because starting salary impacts compensation rates for years to come.

And what about sales? Sobering statistics recently cited by Robert Clay, founder of Marketing Wizdom, showed most of us are going about the selling process the wrong way. People in business often expect to do business the first time they meet a prospect, yet only two percent of sales occur when parties meet for the first time. "The two percent who buy at a first meeting tend to be people who have already looked into the subject matter and already know what they're looking for. If they meet someone who ticks all the right boxes and they get on well, then business may well be transacted. But that is far from the norm. The other 98 percent will only buy once a certain level of trust has been built up," said Clay.

Are most professionals taking the necessary time to grow these relationships? According to Clay, the answer is a resounding no. Although 80 percent of non-routine sales occur only after at least five follow-ups, the vast majority of salespeople (92 percent!) have given up by then. In fact, 44 percent give up after just one "no," and 80 percent of all sales leads are lost due to a lack of follow-up. From these numbers, said Clay, we can infer only eight percent of salespeople are getting 80 percent of the sales. If you have ever tried to sell something, whether it be personal or professional, internal or external, can you say you were in that eight percent?

CHAPTER SUMMARY

- When you provide something that meets a need of your client or customer, you must be able to negotiate for the value you are providing. Be willing to walk away, and know when you must concede for the good of the long-term relationship.
- Everyone is in sales to some degree, even if you are not technically a salesperson. In a sales situation, listen more than you talk and don't sell after the close. Once your prospect has agreed, stop talking.
- Avoid public speaking jitters by rehearsing your opening, getting to the venue early, and finding a friendly face in the audience. Role-playing and improvisation can also be helpful in building your confidence.
- One effective presentation structure is "Tell, Show, Tell." Tell them upfront what you will be presenting, then show them your content, and finally, tell them the key points they should take away.
- When writing a business document, keep your audience in mind and communicate with an appropriate level of formality. Don't get tripped up by spelling errors or commonly misused words.
- Good client service is not saying yes to everything. It's mainly based on empathy. When you understand your client is a person too and you're able to put yourself in their shoes, you're a better partner.

CHAPTER SEVEN

GLOBAL EXPERTISE: MORE THAN STAMPS ON A PASSPORT

When I began my career, it was unusual to have the opportunity to work in another country, or even to work with people from another country. However, the world is becoming increasingly global. More American businesses are engaging overseas, and, according to a recent Mercer report, over half (56 percent) of multinational companies expect to increase the use of short-term international assignments. As the CEO of a multinational organization myself, international issues are on my radar every day. But this certainly wasn't always the case.

When reminiscing about my experience growing up, I once told my mother I felt I grew up in a bubble. I was raised in the suburbs of Long Island, New York, and after college in Massachusetts and a short stint in Manhattan, I settled in a quiet town near where I grew up. I'm not sure whether my college even offered a semester abroad because it was unimaginable to me. I was the kid who got homesick at sleepaway camp, so just being away at college in Massachusetts was enough for me. I don't think I even had a passport until after I was married, and I certainly did not consider myself to be particularly worldly.

I'm also awful at learning and speaking foreign languages, and not for lack of trying. In high school, I got good grades in most things except Spanish. It's like that part of my brain doesn't compute.

My first business trip to Paris in the late 1990s didn't go well. I was flying with a colleague who was a seasoned traveler. We were flying business class and I was so excited I could hardly contain myself. When we met up at JFK Airport, he stopped at McDonalds to get some dinner.

"What are you doing?" I exclaimed. "Don't we get a gourmet dinner and champagne?"

"Oh yeah," he said, "but I like to eat first so that I can go right to sleep. It's not that long a flight, and we have a busy day tomorrow."

Well, not me! I was determined to enjoy every bit of my first international business trip, starting with the flight. Between the meal, the newness of the experience, and the awkwardness of lying next to my snoring colleague, I didn't sleep at all. Once in Paris, things continued to go downhill. I'm a lightweight when it comes to alcohol, but I wanted to fit in and had wine with practically every meal. I didn't pay much attention to the time difference, and I didn't manage my jet lag well at all.

On the flight home, I was a mess. My traveling companion warned me: "Whatever you do, when you get home, don't go to sleep before 9 p.m. local time, or you will never get back on track." Did I listen? No. When I arrived at my house at 4 p.m. (10 p.m. Paris time), I immediately fell into bed. My son Eric, around nine at the time, came into my bedroom with the phone and asked if he could have a playdate. I explained I ate too much rich food, had too much wine, and needed to take a little nap. He said to his friend: "I can't play today, my mom's drunk." You can imagine the damage control I had to do the next day!

My second trip to Paris wasn't much better. This time, I was smarter about eating, drinking, and managing my schedule. Unfortunately, I woke up in my hotel room one morning with my face completely swollen. I must have had an allergic reaction to something. I didn't know what to do! Since it was in the middle of the night in New York, I couldn't call my doctor in the U.S., so I woke my husband and he advised me to get my hands on some Benadryl. I headed out to find a pharmacy. I'll spare you the details, but even after I located the right place, the employees didn't speak English and were generally unhelpful. I got the medicine, but the whole episode left me in tears.

THE AMERICAN AND THE "EUROPEANS"

Given all this, it was a shock when several years later, I was asked to add our European business to my responsibilities. Even though the job didn't require moving, I knew it would necessitate substantial international travel. It was a great opportunity, but I was conflicted and wasn't sure I wanted to do it. Although my children were older and travel wasn't as much of an issue, I was very nervous about such a daunting assignment. I've come to rely on my communication skills and ability to read people, and I wondered if these attributes would serve me the same way outside the U.S. How could I lead when I knew so little about the cultures and business needs of different countries?

But, I'm fortunate to have people in my life who believe in and encourage me. When I called my mother for advice, she was very clear—I'd be crazy to pass up the opportunity. This was a unique chance to expand my horizons. She urged me to look past the concerns and go for it. At this point in my career, I also had a manager who regularly pushed me out of my comfort zone. He recognized I sometimes needed an extra shove to realize my potential. We agreed I would start by joining the task force responsible for hiring our new head of Europe, who would ultimately report to me if I took the position. This would give me a chance to learn more about the region before fully committing to the role. My manager knew once I went over there and engaged, I would see I could do it.

As I got involved with the Europeans, one memorable experience took place during a "Kick off the New Year" meeting in Majorca, Spain. We brought together nearly a hundred people from Europe, including employees from the U.K., Spain, Italy, Germany, and France. At first, I was intimidated. I assumed I was the one who was different. It only took an hour over cocktails to learn there isn't a "Europe!" Each country is unique. They have love-hate relationships with each other just as much as they do with the U.S. I discovered I was just one of six different nationalities and cultures, and while Europeans from different countries have certain things in common, they also have many differences. I also realized you can't stereotype people based on their country and in fact, most often people are just people. Some are extroverts, some are introverts, some are funny, and some are serious. Once I began interacting with each person as an individual and not as a country, my reservations subsided.

Energized, I agreed to take on the leadership role. I knew to be successful, I would have to make a significant commitment.

I confirmed upfront I would have ample budget and time to go to Europe in-person so I could meet the people and learn the business. Taking a page from my own experiences onboarding new employees, I worked with my manager to outline both short-term (learn the job) and longer term (do the job) objectives.

Unlike when I moved from salesperson to sales manager, there wasn't an obvious "off the shelf" course that would address what I needed to learn. So, I crafted my own Global Learning Program. I made a list of people I knew with international work experience and set up a lot of one-on-one meetings. My targets included peers, subordinates, clients, industry colleagues, etc. I then developed some questions to review during my interviews, including the following:

- What advice do you have that will help me be successful in taking on this additional responsibility for our businesses in Europe?
- What books or other resources would you recommend that helped you develop your global skills?
- What mistakes have you made or seen others make that I might avoid?
- Are there other people you recommend I talk with about this?

As I gathered information, I came across several books that became favorites: *French or Foe* by Polly Platt helped me understand the French culture better, and *Kiss, Bow or Shake Hands* by Terri Morrison, a comprehensive review of many cultures, came in especially handy when I took on our Asia-Pacific business a few years later.

My company's head of HR gave me the best piece of advice. She said: "Karyn, you are used to being the leader and directing people. I suggest you relax. Go there, meet as many people as you can, and listen. Don't feel you need to have the answers. Just learn and then you'll know what to do."

Taking her advice, for the next year and a half, I spent one week a month in Western Europe. I went to five countries and met nearly all our staff, either one-on-one or in small groups. I also went to see clients, a suggestion that, ironically, I received from a friendly competitor. This allowed me to understand the external issues and opportunities while also spending time with my teams. And, as my loved ones predicted, it did end up being the learning experience of a lifetime.

Words of Wisdom

"Believe in possibilities and take on every opportunity that comes your way, because you never know what assignment might open the next door."

—Diane Sullivan, CEO, president and chairman of the Board, Caleres.

HELLO, GOODBYE, AND EVERYTHING IN BETWEEN

Since our European headquarters is in France, I thought I should try to learn French. I bought French language tutorial CDs and listened to them in my car for weeks. Unfortunately, I wasn't any better with French than I was with Spanish. For example, I like butter on my bread, and although I tried to say a perfect, "du beurre, s'il vous plait," every waiter would promptly reply, "butter?" I finally realized I was never going to conduct business in fluent French or any other European language, so I committed to learning enough to be polite. Wherever I went, I made it a point to master saying hello and goodbye, which is usually appreciated.

Considering language barriers, nonverbal communication became even more critical. In *French or Foe*, I read that while Americans think it is unfriendly not to smile, people in other countries often think it is odd or phony to smile for no reason. In fact, if you get an ID card to live in Hong Kong, you can't be smiling in your photo! Here's another tip: since I didn't speak the languages, I was nervous about traveling alone in Europe. I learned to have a colleague or someone in the hotel write down the name and directions for where I was going (in the local language) so I didn't have to explain them to a non-English-speaking driver. For return trips, I kept a business card from the hotel on hand to give to the driver.

One of the first times I took a taxi in France, I got confused by the currency. After I got out and the driver left, I realized I had only tipped him the equivalent of 17 cents. I was appalled and mentioned my faux pas to some colleagues. They admonished me, but not for the reason I expected. "Karyn, here we don't tip 10 or 15 percent, we simply round up, so your 17 cents was fine. If all the Americans were to start tipping, it would throw off our economy. Our taxi driver and waiter compensation assumes no tips." Now, whenever I travel to a new country, I check the tipping protocol.

I also had to learn what to call people and how to greet them. I had some funny experiences. One time, I was going with our

French head of Europe to our office in Italy. I had read that in Italy, when greeting someone you know, you kiss once on each cheek, starting on the right. This is the opposite of how you greet a person in France, where you start on the left cheek. To my surprise, our Italian leader greeted the French leader in the French way instead of the Italian way. I asked her about this. Since we were in Italy, shouldn't they be doing it the Italian way? She laughed and said: "Karyn, it doesn't matter that much. The important thing is not to meet in the middle!"

One country that baffled me was England. I was never sure if I should shake hands, kiss once, kiss twice, hug, or what? There were always these awkward few seconds where I didn't know what to do. Interestingly, I read in a book about people in England that this awkward way of greeting is actually very English! The same book also had an entire chapter about the weather and all the reasons talking about the weather is so important to people from England.

While in the U.K., I gave my training class on dealing with difficult client situations. Adding a twist, I brought a variety of small U.K. flags with me and explained participants should raise one of the flags if I said something that didn't make sense or was culturally "off." This way, the class would cover the original topic, but would also address cultural differences. For example, I shared that when giving a client bad news, I often told them I was so worried about the issue that I tried to think through a solution while in the shower, where I do my best thinking. Immediately, all of the flags went waving. "Here in England, we never talk about what we do in the shower," they laughed. We decided they could tell the client they were thinking about the issue on their commute to work instead!

While on the subject of cultural sensitivities, let's talk about Canada for a moment. Just because people in a certain country live close by or speak the same language, it doesn't mean they are the same. Canadians rightfully get very offended when Americans insinuate Canada is akin to a 51st state of the U.S.

An acquaintance told me her company reorganized to put Australia, the U.K., Canada, and the U.S. into a common region under one manager. This is an interesting strategy based on the shared English language, but it overlooks that these are very different countries and cultures. In my company, we once decided to have many functions in Canada report to the U.S. It seemed like a good idea at the time, but there were unintended consequences. For example, when we conducted quarterly business reviews in Toronto, so many people from the U.S. attended that we had more Americans present than Canadians! The American managers were each only spending a small amount of time on the Canadian business, which wasn't effective. And most importantly, we lost the heart and soul of our Canadian office. Ultimately, we hired a Canadian leader and restructured so that Canadian functions report into Canada. As for me, I gained a new respect for our neighbors to the north and their unique history, government, laws, and heritage.

A TRUE FOREIGNER IN APAC

APAC (Asia Pacific) was in some ways tougher for me than Western Europe, but in other ways easier. In most parts of Europe, it wasn't obvious I was from somewhere else, so my lack of knowledge, cultural mores, and language skills made me feel out of place. In most parts of Asia, there was no question I was an outsider. On my first trip to the region, the only other tall blonde woman I saw over two weeks was a mannequin in a store window!

The ritual of exchanging business cards in parts of Asia, while awkward at first, is one I have come to admire. It is a formal and civilized process whereby you face your card toward the other person and present it to them with both hands. As a sign of respect, you study the other person's card slowly and carefully note their name and title. If you are sitting at a table, it is customary to place the card or cards in front of you, face up, for the duration of the meeting. After spending time in Asia, I was disappointed to hand my business card to someone in the U.S., only to have them shove it in their pocket without as much as a glance.

It took me a while to learn the proper etiquette for various situations when doing business in APAC. For example, in Japan, if you stand facing backwards, or dare to speak in an elevator, people will think you are crazy. At one company I visited, there was even a sign in the elevator that said: "Silence, please." My colleague, Jim, who lived in Asia for a time, shared an amusing etiquette difference that, fortunately, I didn't personally experience. He explained it is common to pass gas freely, loudly, and sometimes proudly at any time and place in Asia. Although the belief that it's better to "let it out than hold it in" is both healthy and practical, you can imagine how awkward the practice might be for a reserved westerner standing nearby!

As for meal etiquette, one of my more memorable dining experiences was in South Korea. We were having dinner with the president and executive team of a well-known Korean manufacturer. There are specific customs when dining out in Korea, starting with the seating. At a long, rectangular table, the most senior people sit facing each other at the center of the table, with the remaining people sitting on both sides of the highest-ranking individuals in order of seniority. The hosts sit on the side closest to the door. Since I was the most senior person from our side, I sat opposite the president. I had learned in advance no one eats until the senior person starts. I'd also practiced the right way to pour a drink for my host, using two hands after he did the same for me.

While senior women in business are currently uncommon in Korea, I was pleasantly surprised at how respectful the Korean executives were to me, and we had a pleasant evening. I was a bit of an anomaly to them, especially when we got on the subject of cooking. Apparently, in Korea, male executives work late into the night and usually have dinner with their colleagues. In fact, they joked a "good Korean husband" only comes home once or twice during the week. This is because when they do, it is an ordeal for their wives. They explained their presence required their wives to go to the market to buy fresh food and spend most of the day preparing a big dinner. The executives were perplexed—if I was working every day, who made dinner for my husband and me?

NAVIGATING OVERSEAS MORAL QUANDARIES

If asked "Are you a truthful person?" most people will say "Yes, of course." But we are also comfortable "spinning" a story to get our point across, or telling a small fib, especially if we are trying to avoid hurting someone's feelings, as in: "Don't be silly, your new haircut looks just fine." We even have a word for this: a "white lie." But how do you draw the line between a white lie and a real lie? Are there shades of grey? To my surprise, the lines between truths, fibs, and lies can differ between cultures. Just using words like "truth" and "lie" can create ill will. Working internationally, I've learned I can't assume my moral compass is the only one, and sometimes I have to be flexible in my thinking.

When dealing with people around the world and speaking in English, it's also important to remember they aren't just talking with an accent—they are talking in a language that often isn't their primary one! It's not fair to judge someone harshly if their communication isn't crystal clear. Particularly if you are presenting or talking on the phone, speak slowly and paraphrase back what you heard to ensure comprehension. Just because someone is nodding doesn't mean they agree with you or even understand you. Without being rude, you might ask the person to confirm what they heard in their own words so you can check the effectiveness of the exchange.

Although tolerance is important, there are times when you simply can't adhere to local customs. My company follows U.S. accounting and legal principles, which can make doing business in certain parts of the world challenging. Bribery and embezzlement may be common practices in some regions, but that doesn't mean you should take part. When starting a business in one of the BRIMC countries (Brazil, Russia, India, Mexico, and China), for instance, my company had all the partners signed up and ready to launch. At the last minute, we were forced to abort our plans because we found out one of our partners was engaged in financial practices that were illegal in the U.S. Fortunately, this was an exception, and we have had several other successful ventures in this country.

A friend told me a story about a situation in another BRIMC country. She thought her company had contracted to receive information from Company X. When my friend got involved in the region, she checked all the contracts and found there wasn't one in place for Company X. She discovered that one of her employees had been taking company cash in a lunchbox and meeting up with a Company X employee to exchange the cash for the information without approval from Company X leadership. The employee was fired and the practice discontinued. The message is: what's perfectly acceptable behavior in foreign countries may not fly in a North American-based company. When in doubt, check it out!

WHEN YOU GO THERE, GO THERE

As my passport filled up with stamps from countries around the world, I started to treasure these new and exciting experiences. However, it took me a while to truly appreciate and make the most of them. For example, when asked if I've ever been to Geneva, I struggle with the answer. Technically, I have been to Geneva, but I was never *really* there. I flew in one day for a conference. It was raining so I went directly to the conference center. Aside from the drive to and from the airport, I never left that building. I didn't get to see the Cathedrale de St Pierre or the famous Jet d'Eau fountain. I could have been in New Jersey! As soon as I returned home and realized this missed opportunity, I decided it would never happen again.

If you are fortunate enough to travel for business, use it to increase your exposure to the world. Leave a day early or stay a day late, whatever works, but make sure you carve out time to see a new city and taste a different way of life. And if you cannot do that, ask your local hosts about their city and their culture.

I really got the hang of this when I headed to Barcelona, Spain. Barcelona is a lovely seaside city with boundless culture, unique architecture, and a world-class drinking and dining scene. I was at a conference, but during a session that was not relevant to me, I asked a colleague if he wanted to go for a walk. Ted and I had worked together for years, but we had never socialized. We had the most lovely and memorable afternoon walking through the city, taking in the beautiful architecture, and stopping in a small museum. On the heels of Barcelona, I went to Madrid. Though I had a packed schedule, my co-worker Leon and I managed to enjoy some sangria at the Plaza Mayor. The special Spanish drink made me feel as though I had experienced a touch of Madrid.

It's also fun if you can pick something small to collect on your business travels. The snow globe collection I started for my son, Eric, gave me an excuse to get out and explore other countries. Even my traveling companions often got in the spirit trying to find the most interesting globes for my son.

THE CASE(S) OF THE MISSING PASSPORT

When you are preparing to travel out of the country on business, having a valid passport and/or visa may be the last thing you're thinking about. You'll find, however, you can't get very far without the necessary travel documents! If you are traveling overseas, it is a good practice to take photos of important documents and carry them in a different place than the originals. You might also get an ATM card that works around the world and keep local currency on hand. Finally, if a country requires a visa, such as China or Brazil, watch out for the dates. Don't be fooled into thinking it only takes a few days to get one. The process can be lengthy, and sometimes you need a passport that is valid for at least six months or more before you can get a visa. Be sure to check the country you are visiting well in advance to understand what is needed.

I have had a few bad experiences involving passports, including forgetting it twice. Once, I embarked on an extensive North American trip to Houston, San Diego, Chicago, Greensboro, and Toronto. Remember when I said my company once muddied the waters between the U.S. and Canada? Well, when planning and packing for the trip, I actually forgot Toronto is in another country! I got quite the ribbing from my colleagues. Fortunately, back then you could still use your driver's license to move between the U.S. and Canada, so I was able to continue the trip, but that has changed now and you definitely need your passport.

I'm not sure where to place the blame for the other time I forgot my passport. Ever since I started traveling for business, I've kept my passport in a pink passport holder. But during a family trip to the Caribbean, my husband had removed my passport from the holder. Weeks later, when I was packing for a trip to Europe, I grabbed the holder from its locked drawer and headed to the airport. The passport holder alone wasn't going to get me through security, however! To avoid missing the flight, I called a taxi to go to my house and pick up my actual passport. The expense was enormous, but the worst part was having to wait uncomfortably with my boss and co-workers not knowing if I was going to make it or not. I did make it, but just in the nick of time!

A colleague, Wanda, lost her passport while we were in Spain. She looked everywhere—her briefcase, her purse, and her suitcase—to no avail. In order to get home, Wanda spent a whole afternoon at the U.S. Embassy in Madrid, which was a major hassle. It would have been easier if she had her passport number with her. Months later, Wanda found her missing passport. It had fallen into the lining of her suitcase!

SIX BASICS FOR WORKING ON A GLOBAL TEAM

#1: Be culturally curious. In a recent survey by RW3/Culture Wizard, 48 percent of professionals working at companies with international business activity said more than half of their organization's teams include members from other countries.

Working effectively on a global or multi-country team starts with being culturally aware. Simple things like saying "hello" instead of "good morning" when it is evening to the other person shows you are mindful of differences. It helps to start calls with a warm greeting in the other person's language. Even if you have to use a translation service to help, a cheery "hola" or "shalom" can go a long way.

When working with colleagues from another country for the first time, spend a lot of time listening and asking questions about work-related mores. For example, in some cultures, it is impolite to jump right into business without sufficient small talk. In others, decision-making will be a more involved process. A friend told me when she first sat in predominantly French meetings, she thought her colleagues were trying to avoid making a decision, when in reality, they wanted to make a thoughtful and wise one. Thoroughness was valued over speed.

#2: Slow down. Remember when you're speaking in English, slow down! Especially if you are on the phone, it's hard to follow a discussion even when everyone speaks the same language. Be sure to engage in two-way dialogue so everyone understands what was said and follow up with meeting notes confirming the messages.

#3: Check the clock. Be sensitive to time zone differences. Try to avoid setting up calls or meetings that are outside your global colleagues' regular work schedule. If these are necessary, take turns so your colleagues aren't always the ones inconvenienced by having to get up early or stay up late.

When sending meeting invites, include all the relevant time zones. Personally, I find using Eastern Standard Time and Daylight Savings Time confusing because different regions don't always change at the same time. For example, depending on the time of year, sometimes New York and Paris have a six hour time difference and sometimes they have a five hour time difference. In order avoid confusion, be more specific (e.g., 7 a.m. NY time, 1 p.m. (13:00) Paris time).

#4: Beware of date and currency confusion. You should also be conscious of differences in nomenclature and currency. For example, when writing out a date, 4/9/17 could either be April 9 or September 4. Avoid potential misunderstandings by writing out the full date: April 9, 2017. Similarly, be careful about always talking in dollars, instead recognizing other currencies. If working with multi-country financials or analyses, it is essential to know which currency you are dealing in, and if necessary, what exchange rates were used.

#5: Leverage in-person opportunities. If you have the opportunity to meet your global teammates in-person, take advantage of this and try to set aside some time for relationship building. Face-to-face interaction, particularly over a meal, is especially important when working alongside people from other countries. Even one in-person meeting can change all future interactions for the better.

#6: Eat, drink, and be merry! Meals present an opportunity to bond, but can be an area of conflict if you are not careful. In the U.S., we think nothing of eating in the car or doing business over lunch. In other countries, lunch is a time to relax and enjoy the food and each other's company.

My co-worker Kerry told me a funny story about when she went to Australia, where they have a great coffee culture. Many business meetings take place over coffee. These are casual and most coffee places have outdoor seating. Kerry showed up in a full suit for her first coffee meeting, which was in the middle of the summer. The client used her Aussie humor to let Kerry know she didn't need to be so stuffy for a coffee meeting. Thank goodness the client encouraged Kerry to take off her jacket so she wouldn't melt!

FINDING WORK OVERSEAS

As you're reading, maybe the prospect of working overseas or with global colleagues appeals to you. If you haven't yet had an opportunity but would like one, be proactive! If your company does business in other countries, make it known you are open to moving for either a short or long-term stint. You'll need to consider how long an assignment makes sense for you. Most expat assignments average three years, but there are certainly exceptions. In my company, we have had several three to nine month assignments designed to fill in for someone on a leave of absence.

You will be a more attractive candidate if you speak the local language, but this doesn't need to be a barrier either. Excelling at your current role, and having a unique skill or knowledge area, will put you in a better position to be considered. How you interact with others on a global team or task force will also indicate to your management team how well you would do on an international assignment. You want to be perceived as being culturally sensitive and open to different perspectives. Finally, you should assess your motives. If you are going primarily to get a free trip to an exotic new locale, think twice. Expat assignments are hard work and require a full commitment to the position, the new culture, and the company.

PLANNING TO LIVE AND WORK ABROAD

I tapped three of my colleagues who lived and worked abroad to share some of their most useful tips. Heidi, Kerry, and Jim represent a good cross-section, since their assignments spanned France, Central America, Australia, and Asia. Heidi is a product development and marketing executive, Kerry specializes in client service, and Jim is a general manager.

Heidi had this to say: "If you have the opportunity to live or travel overseas, do it! Even if it is scary or hard. Fear is very common as one is preparing to embark on something like this, and one may look for many excuses why we cannot. Oliver Wendell Holmes Jr. said: 'A mind that is stretched by a new experience can never go back to its old dimensions.' As someone who has lived in six countries and traveled to well over 40, few experiences in life stretch the mind like international experience."

While many people may travel extensively, there is a big difference between living in a region and just visiting. My colleagues advised doing your research on the country and the culture and getting the documents and living plans in place in advance. When negotiating your package to move or work internationally, talk to others who have done it before. Be clear on work visa and tax rules before you go. There is a lot to learn about what you should receive and what might be above the norm, and you should aim for a package equitable for both parties. Consider negotiating for living expenses and tax equalization with your employer. If living oversees for a year or less, try to get paid in your home country currency and keep your home country bank. There is no need to open a local account. Repatriating money at the end of your tour is more painful than one might think. Multi-year assignments, however, usually require a local bank for logistical issues such as taxes and housing. As for credit cards, "get one with no fees on international charges," recommended Heidi. "Set up a cloud services account to back up your files and photos since living overseas may increase your likelihood of losing cell phones and PCs. And on the topic of your phone, if you are living overseas for six months or more, consider a local phone."

"Also, despite so much being online these days, some things still come via mail and international mail forwarding is not terribly timely," Heidi said. "If you can, have home country mail sent to trusted family members or friends. Determine a secure cloud location for them to upload scanned sensitive documents rather than send via email."

All three of my globe-trotting co-workers talked about the importance of ensuring any family members going with you are comfortable with the move. The happiness of your family and/or partner will make or break your success with the job and experience of living abroad. Getting your family settled should be your first priority, and often the burden of day to day logistics falls on them.

Jim and his partner struggled initially when they moved to Hong Kong for Jim's job. They were in a new country, didn't speak the language, and Jim was traveling a great deal. Being a same sex couple in the Far East added to the complexity of adjusting. At first, Jim's partner was miserable. My friend Lisa had been living in Hong Kong for three years, and after an introduction over dinner, she connected Jim and his partner to the expat community. Jim's partner started making friends and began to feel like the new city was home. Jim said: "Having my partner with me in Asia made it a shared adventure that significantly enhanced my experience, satisfaction, and overall happiness living in numerous time zones and thousands of miles away in a foreign land. We were in this together and shared the challenges of being western in the Far East."

What else can you do to make the most of your international experience? "Expect to be out of your comfort zone often and don't take yourself too seriously," said Heidi. "Working in a foreign place can be intimidating. Take your ego out of the experience and be willing to laugh at yourself. Assume you will misinterpret some situations and make some faux pas, and this is okay! Try new foods: if nothing else, this makes for great stories later." Heidi is right. I am especially proud to say when I was in Australia, I tried crocodile and kangaroo, all while taking a camel ride under the stars!

"Embrace the experience," Kerry said. "Travel, explore, and immerse yourself in the culture. You should work hard, but take the time to enjoy it as well. Don't be afraid of the friend date. If you have a friend of a friend who knows someone in the same city you will be living, take the time to have dinner with that person. You might just meet your new best friend!"

She went on to say: "Keep in mind that traveling and living in a new country is like being invited into someone's home. If the rule is to remove one's shoes at the door, one does so. You are a guest in another country and it is good manners to do as the locals do even if it feels strange to you." Jim added: "Dress the part too. For example, in Japan and Korea, it is important for a man to wear a tie, especially if he is meeting someone senior to him."

DID YOU KNOW?

The term "expat" derives from the Latin prefix *ex* (out of) and the noun *patria* (home country, native country, or fatherland). The word is generally used to refer to people who temporarily or permanently live in a different country than the one they were born in or whose nationality they have. Expats usually choose to leave their native country for a career boost or to fulfill a personal dream or goal, rather than as a result of dire economic necessity.

According to the *InterNations* online community, although the term "expat" is often used to describe highly-qualified employees who take up a foreign assignment or work at a foreign branch office of their company for several months or years, there are also so-called "serial expats," who move from one country to another on a series of international assignments. And not all expats are employees; some people move abroad to work as freelancers or open up a business in a foreign country.

Typically, American expats are highly educated and enjoy a higher than average income. But many face language barriers and culture shock, as well as having to contend with new standards of living if they relocate from an industrial nation to a developing country.

Words of Wisdom

"Be curious and explore. Talk to other people about their jobs, what they do, what they love about their roles—and what they don't. Don't get boxed into a position or function too quickly. Search for the job that taps your passion and gets you excited!"

—Barb Murrer, insights lead, Levi Strauss & Co.

LOCAL BUSINESS SAVVY

Heidi suggested if you have to arrange a business dinner or event, leverage a local colleague to select the location and manage logistics. They will know better what is appropriate. Additionally, depending on where you are going, you might bring some small gifts from home. They come in handy as gifts for your hosts, or for the first time you are in your company's local office.

Jim also recommended you plan to arrive 30 minutes early for any and all meetings in your new city. Getting around in a foreign country can be a challenge, whether it is navigating via mass transit or a taxi, and in most countries (especially in Asia), being punctual is a required business practice.

My colleagues also discussed the importance of staying connected to your home office even as you bond with new co-workers. Kerry said when she moved to Australia, she woke up early or worked late so she could talk live to her American co-workers (using video chat when possible). This activity helped grow Kerry's personal brand within the company and build relationships with others she might not have known living in the same country. She set up times to talk during their business hours since she was usually asking for or needing something from them. Finally, Kerry suggested asking for conference calls or webinars (where your live participation is not mandatory) to be recorded.

FORGING NEW FRIENDSHIPS AND MINIMIZING STRESS

All three of these travelers talked about the importance of building relationships, which as you know by now, is one of my favorite topics! In many foreign countries, work collaboration is more effective after you have built a relationship. In most cultures, it's okay to ask questions about the country and the person. This is a good way to get to know someone. American TV shows, music, and movies are not as likely to be relevant outside the U.S., so think about other topics of conversation. If language and culture are barriers, bridge the gap by bringing a picture of your family or home to the office and sharing information about your hobbies.

While living in Australia, Kerry and her husband hosted an American-style Thanksgiving. They invited their Australian friends and made the typical Thanksgiving day foods as best they could. "We had to go to the butcher to special order a turkey," Kerry said. "Yes, it was expensive, but well worth the effort. We had to make pumpkin pie and sweet potato casserole from actual pumpkin and sweet potatoes and not from the canned/tinned versions. These don't exist in Australia. Our guests were cautious when first trying these, but very excited the following year to have pumpkin pie again. Sharing something American brought us closer to our Australian friends."

As you adjust to life in a new land, there are many things you can do to decrease your stress level all around. Depending on your length of stay, my colleagues advised, you may want to request language tutoring. At a minimum, try to learn enough to have a basic, polite conversation even if you can't actively engage in the host language. Heidi recommended Duolingo, a free app that makes learning the basics fairly fun.

Unfortunately, the world is becoming a scarier place, and while this shouldn't deter you from traveling, you want to be smart about it. Check the state department pages for that country and ask the locals about safety. Trust your instincts. "When I was living in Mexico City, the head of the U.S. Embassy's security team told me almost everyone who had a problem said something felt off right before the incident happened. He said if you feel that way, cross the street or get away from the situation immediately," said Heidi.

THE GLOBAL JOURNEY

I'm grateful my international work experiences have helped me lead in a more globally inclusive way. I regularly remind my U.S. colleagues best practices go both ways and there are just as many things we can learn from people in other regions as they can learn from us.

In putting together a recent meeting, which I was hosting for colleagues from around the world, I tried to be globally-minded. I created a multi-country task force to come up with creative ideas to raise awareness around our global colleagues and markets. We served food from different countries, held a "high tea" instead of a coffee break, used icons instead of having the signage in English, and interspersed different languages for common words such as "Agenda," "Breakfast," and "Break Time."

Another example involves a man from my company who tried to make his French remarks more accessible to an American audience with a comical presentation that exclusively used words most of us were familiar with—like chauffeur, fiancé, faux pas, chic, and déjà vu.

While at the podium kicking off the day's activities, I said "hello" and "good morning" in a different language every day. My international colleagues really appreciated the effort, and I never would have had the right perspective if not for my years in the overseas trenches!

OVERSEAS FAUX PAS

"I learned the hard way not to wear outdoor shoes to the gym. Gyms in Japan require that you bring a different pair of shoes to the gym than those you wear *into* the gym. Otherwise you have to rent indoor shoes. I spent 10 minutes at the counter of the gym trying to convince the manager that my shoes were indoor shoes even though I had just walked in the door with them on. I then walked outside the gym, took them off, put them in my backpack, and was able to enter the gym." Jim

"I was learning Spanish in Central America, and I was trying to explain what I had learned that day to a much respected local matriarch over dinner. In Spanish, one says: "I have hunger," or "I have fear," instead of "I am hungry," or "I am afraid." Instead of saying "Tengo miedo" (I have fear) of spiders, I said "Tengo mierda," or "I have sh*t." Heidi

"In China, we were having a very heated internal meeting. I knew the team well, but let my American-ness take over. I pointed my finger a few times. Finally, one of my coworkers grabbed my hand, placed it on the table, and asked me to please stop pointing. I try my best not to be culturally insensitive, so I chose to make fun of myself. I called myself the ugly American and apologized. We all laughed, and I am more conscious of pointing my finger now, even in the U.S." Kerry

"During one trip to Japan, I was booked solid with meetings in different parts of Tokyo. One day, we had not booked time for lunch and only had one hour in transit to get from one meeting to another. So, being American, I decided to buy some food in the train station and eat it on the train to my next meeting. I arrived on the train happy to get a seat. I opened my bag of food and proceeded to enjoy my lunch. After a few minutes, I noticed the train was very quiet, and many if not all of the Japanese people were staring at me, some in horror. I realized that I had broken cultural etiquette and quietly pushed my sandwich back into the bag." Jim

SURVEY SAYS: WHERE WE'RE GOING AND WHAT WE'RE DOING

Regardless of who you ask, you will hear international mobility is exploding. Twenty-first century globalization is, of course, a major factor. However, interest from millennial professionals who now make up the majority of the workforce is at play as well. According to recent research from PricewaterhouseCoopers, over 70 percent of millennials would like to try living in a new country as they advance their careers. PwC found short-term, international assignments are expected to make up about 20 percent of corporate relocations, representing a 100 percent increase over the past 10 years.

A second study featured in Mercer's *Worldwide Survey of International Assignment Policies and Practices* report found, over the next several years, around half of companies anticipate an increase in the use of permanent transfers (54 percent), developmental and training assignments (50 percent), and locally hired foreigners (47 percent). A smaller proportion of respondents (44 percent) expects to see a rise in more traditional long-term assignments.

The top five drivers behind international assignments were to provide specific technical skills not available locally (47 percent), to ensure know-how transfer (43 percent), to provide specific managerial skills (41 percent), to facilitate career management and leadership development (41 percent), and to fulfill specific project needs (40 percent).

Mercer also found two-thirds of long-term assignees (66 percent) are between 35-55 years old, whereas short-term assignees increasingly fall into the under 35 bracket (48 percent). Interestingly, the proportion of female expatriates has increased from previous years, with the worldwide average participation at 15 percent and rising quickly.

According to a LinkedIn study, English-speaking countries are most popular for relocation, with London, Sydney, and Melbourne taking the top spots. In terms of which U.S. cities tend to be springboards for international assignments, it won't surprise you Washington, DC is first, followed by New York, Austin, Boston, and surprisingly, the Midwestern college town of Bloomington, Indiana! LinkedIn also found industries that are particularly well-suited to international assignments include education, translation, marketing, and consulting.

Although this chapter focused mostly on corporate expatriates, an intriguing study by a global collaboration of researchers including Vance, McNulty, Paik, and D'Mello highlighted a growing category termed "expat-preneurs." The researchers defined expat-preneurs as individuals who start a new business in a host country, or join local host-country entrepreneurial activities. Some are so-called pre-departure expat-preneurs, who move abroad with a preconceived entrepreneurial purpose, while others try to expand their business from their home country to a new location. Some expat-preneurs develop entrepreneurial intentions while working for a company abroad, eventually deciding to leave and start up their own business in the host location. These individuals are called transitioned expat-preneurs.

Expat-preneurs differ from traditional expats in a variety of ways. First, attracted by the potential of new market opportunities in the local economy, expat-preneurs do not require any additional incentives or foreign-scaled salaries for agreeing to go and work abroad. Expat-preneurs come willingly, out of their own initiative, at their own cost, and typically ready to be paid on a local scale. Also, they are often better adjusted because they possess a more solid understanding of the local environment due to their previous work experience and time spent in the host location. Finally, pre-departure expat-preneurs are potentially better equipped for relocation, as planning an entrepreneurial endeavor usually entails thorough background checks and preparation.

CHAPTER SUMMARY

- There may not be an obvious way to prepare for an overseas work assignment. Consider creating your own Global Learning Program instead. Make a list of people you know with international work experience and interview them one-on-one for their tips and advice.
- Become proficient in the basics of the language of the country in which you are working, knowing enough to greet people and be polite. Master cultural nuances related to meetings and meals, and where it's ethical to do so, adhere to local business customs.
- If you are fortunate to have the chance to travel for business, use it to increase your exposure to the world. Leave a day early or stay a day late, but make sure you carve out time to see a new city and taste a different way of life.
- Working effectively on a global or multi-country team starts with being culturally aware. Be mindful of time differences and language barriers, and meet in-person when possible to strengthen relationships.
- When working overseas, you don't need to be deterred by danger, but you should be smart and trust your instincts. Enlist the help of local colleagues to get where you need to go safely, and if something seems off, remove yourself from the situation.
- If you haven't yet had an opportunity to work internationally but find it appealing, be proactive! If your company does

business in other countries, make it known you are open to moving for either a short or long-term stint.

CHAPTER EIGHT

LEADERSHIP: INSPIRING OTHERS TO FOLLOW YOU

Leadership is commonly described as a process of social influence in which one person can enlist others to accomplish a common goal. Done correctly, it's about harnessing the power of the team to do extraordinary things.

Anyone can be a leader, regardless of level or amount of experience. For example, my executive assistant is clearly a leader. She is responsible for most of our internal corporate events, and, as such, takes charge of every last detail with minimal supervision. Similarly, junior staff members can take on leadership roles by volunteering to head up an activity committee or an internal task force. While much of this chapter focuses on senior leadership and you may not yet be at that stage, understanding what makes a good leader can help you evaluate your own skills and begin internalizing those you will need to be successful.

While leaders will often still need to manage, there are differences between leading and managing. In his book, *You Don't Need a Title to be a Leader*, Mark Sanborn compared the two as follows:

Management	Leadership
Managers have employees	Leaders win followers
Managers react to change	Leaders create change
Managers have good ideas	Leaders implement good ideas
Managers communicate	Leaders persuade
Managers direct groups	Leaders create teams
Managers try to be heroes	Leaders make heroes out of everyone
Managers take credit	Leaders take responsibility
Managers exercise power over people	Leaders exercise power with people

Earlier in my career, I progressed through a variety of positions. I was a project director, a salesperson, a sales manager, and the head of client service and sales. For much of this time, I reported to the president of my division, who was very supportive and gave me great guidance and advice. But, I wasn't sure what she did as the president. I remember wondering: since she didn't have clients or her own sales goal, what did she actually do all day?

When I switched divisions and was promoted to a business unit president, I was concerned. Now that I was a president, what would I do differently? How would my role change? I certainly didn't want to be just a figurehead. Fortunately, my manager sent me to a four-day leadership course from The Presidents Association (PA). This organization's definition of leadership is "the ability to influence people to follow willingly in pursuit of a common goal." During the course, I learned that as a leader, I would spend my time on different things than I had in the past. The PA's framework covers five areas of leadership, including planning, culture, developing people, organizing, and metrics. I was energized.

As you know by now, I like lists and used them again in this situation to change how I spent my time. I organized my to-dos around the five areas of leadership described in the PA course. If something didn't fall into one of those buckets, I either delegated it or didn't do it. For example, I once liked selecting the incentive gifts we would give people for completing long surveys. I love shopping, so this was a fun thing for me to do. However, it was no longer an appropriate use of my time, so I transitioned the responsibility to a staff member who had a similar passion for this task. Over the years, I've developed my own adjustments to the PA framework, but I still refer to it to ensure I'm spending my time appropriately as a leader.

Words of Wisdom

"Leadership is a state of mind, not a title or box on an org chart. Take responsibility for moving things forward and you will be amazed at how many people follow you!"

—Karen Fichuk, global president, Nielsen.

COMMUNICATING A VISION

Leaders define the organization's values and shape its culture. As a leader, part of my responsibility is to inspire people to believe in our vision and want to be a part of it. I like to position this in terms of what the vision means for our company, clients, and employees, because it's important people understand how the vision affects them and what they can do to contribute. Frequent and motivating communication is key, but just communicating it isn't enough. I need to walk the walk.

For example, when my company decided to become a more customer-centric organization—offering solutions instead of just data—I wanted to personally demonstrate what this meant. Our strategy involved getting in front of executive-level clients and uncovering their business issues rather than just their research problems. I led by example, visiting over 50 clients worldwide in a three-month period. My team and I took pictures with the clients and documented examples of the new things we were talking about. I encouraged others to do the same, and we shared the case studies and photos on the company intranet. Before we knew it, everyone was talking more about clients' business issues and actually getting out of the office to hear from customers.

While we're on the subject of changing a vision: although it is essential to be flexible and to adapt to new technology or competition, leaders should avoid a "vision du jour" or "strategy du jour" that changes too frequently. Both your organization and your people will be better off with a consistent message everyone has agreed to and is committed to acting upon.

BUILDING A VIBRANT CULTURE

"Culture eats strategy for breakfast" is a famous quotation attributed to the late business management guru Peter Drucker. Culture refers to the customs, beliefs, and attitudes that make the organization what it is. The culture should reflect the core values of the company and the leader's behavior should reflect the culture. If the leader wants a very hard driven, high performance culture, they should reward people who demonstrate this behavior.

For instance, some investment banks and law firms bring on a large number of interns or entry level employees, making it clear not everyone will be invited to stay permanently. This drives a strong performance culture, as well as a very competitive one. Conversely, if a leader values collaboration, then people who work well on teams should be recognized. A strong culture, regardless of what kind, gives employees direction on how to behave. If a new employee isn't a good cultural fit, their chance of success is greatly diminished, and even the most logical business acquisitions can go terribly wrong if the cultures are mismatched.

My friend worked for a small, progressive advertising agency and loved her job. All the employees were proud of their culture. Valuing creativity, collaboration, and balance, they spent a lot of time interviewing candidates and talking about the culture to ensure the right fit. Because the company was private, leaders were able to focus on the long-term vision and not just on short-term financial performance. When the company was acquired by a large public conglomerate, initially the leaders were told the firm would stay independent and be able to maintain its culture. However, as time passed, the new management wanted a higher return on investment and short-term financial margins became more important than creativity and collaboration. Open positions weren't approved and voluntary turnover increased. All in all, the firm was no longer a cultural fit for my friend and ultimately she quit, along with some of her similarly-minded colleagues.

There are many kinds of organizational cultures, and there isn't a right or wrong one. But it's the leader's job to understand what makes the organization's culture special. If you are new, one of the best ways to learn about corporate culture is to talk with lots of people to ascertain the behaviors that are rewarded and discouraged. Paying attention to who gets promoted and who is moved aside will also offer you good insight into the culture.

Maintaining a culture takes effort, and changing it is difficult and certainly doesn't happen overnight. But successful companies sometimes need to shake things up to remain competitive and not become complacent. I faced this challenge when my company needed to bring in new skills and thinking to achieve its growth objectives. In this case, it was necessary to get people out of their comfort zone. Internally, we talked about our strategy a great deal, letting people know to remain successful, we had to make certain changes. During orientation, I gave new senior employees a small wooden sailboat that said: "It's okay to rock the boat," which served as a reminder they were hired to help us make changes.

ENCOURAGING DIFFERENT PERSPECTIVES

I was once asked a very odd question: "What role does sharing the rationale for your vision play in getting people on board, and how do you overcome different perspectives based on different experiences and biases?" The first part is easy, but the second part of the question had me perplexed. Why would I want to *overcome* different perspectives? I explained embracing different perspectives makes for a much richer discussion and better ultimate outcome.

I belong to an organization called the CEO Connection. A few years ago, I attended one of their boot camps for c-level executives.

The instructor talked about the best way to build an effective c-suite team. Top leaders' responsibilities include strategy, people, and finance. Not every leader is equally good at all three, so one should build a team around what is needed. For example, if the Chairman is less strong in dealing with people, they will need an excellent head of HR, while if the CEO is less strong in finance, they will need an excellent CFO. I believe leadership can be a team sport. I like the William Wrigley quote about two men who always agree.

William Wrigley Jr. built a company and a fortune by selling chewing gum in the U.S. and around the world. In 1931, Wrigley was interviewed in the *American Magazine* and stated he preferred an employee with a backbone who was willing to challenge him and sometimes tell him, "I think you're wrong."

"Business is built by men who care," said Wrigley in the article. "They care enough to disagree, fight it out to a finish, get facts. When two men always agree, one of them is unnecessary." Logitech CEO Bracken Darrell expressed much the same sentiment in the *New York Times.* "Be sure to tell the boss what's wrong," he said. "The most dangerous thing is to be sitting in an office and nobody's telling you what's wrong. So [when I started at Logitech], I immediately started talking about speaking up and moving fast."

MARCHING TO THE SAME BEAT

While different perspectives are essential, it is also critical the leadership team is aligned on the best path forward. Imagine a bunch of leaders are on a dogsledding team. If everyone is pulling in different directions, the sled won't go anywhere. On the other hand, if they are pointing in the same direction, they can move forward even when engaged in separate but related tasks.

An important first step is to establish who the decision-maker is versus who is providing input. My company had an issue with this in our executive meetings because people thought they had a vote in a decision, when in fact the Chairman was making the final call. To avoid confusion and frustration, we changed our process to be more transparent.

Along these same lines, I once had a coworker who said to people: "You're not listening to me." This was not exactly true. Our colleagues were listening, they just weren't agreeing. As a leader, I work to ensure people's points of view are heard and digested. I paraphrase back what they said, and if I am not able to incorporate their point of view into my thinking, I explain why we are going in a different direction. I spend the extra effort to encourage buy-in so everyone in the room walks out united.

Let's explore the concept of alignment in greater detail. When there's no consensus but a lot of conviction, Amazon founder and CEO Jeff Bezos has this advice: "disagree and commit." My friend and chief executive of Cambridge International Group, Saj-nicole Joni, said alignment describes your level of commitment to the implementation of a decision, regardless of whether you agreed with it in the first place. Without the fuel of alignment, execution is simply not sustainable. Joni and her colleague Dan Arnoudese developed a simple scale from +3 to -3 to describe degrees of alignment among team members.

Owners (+3). These visionary team members show no matter what positions they advocated in the discussions leading up to the decision, they are now committed advocates. They work hard to align others and remove barriers.

Buy-inners (+2). These implementers are personally committed but not enrollers of others. You can count on them to personally do their parts in implementing the plan but not to be active in generating broad support for it across the organization.

Compliers (+1). These implementers are good soldiers who go along with the decision and do what they are told without opposing things. But, don't expect a lot of enthusiasm or extra effort from them.

Abstainers (-1). These people are hands off. They refuse to take a position either way, remaining neutral and uninvolved.

Passive resisters (-2). These people work in stealth mode to sow uncertainty about the decision through rumormongering and backroom chatter. But they leave no fingerprints and can't be linked to public resistance.

Saboteurs (-3). These people fight back openly, opposing the plan and doing whatever it takes to kill it before it sees the light of day.

As a leader, some members of your team will sit above the line while others will fall below it, but according to Joni and Arnoudese, your goal should be to move all team members to a +2 or a +3.

DELEGATING WITH APLOMB

From your very first promotion, you need to delegate so you aren't spending time on tasks you are no longer being paid to do. There are two factors necessary for delegation: someone who is willing to throw the ball and someone who is willing to catch it. You need to find the right person for the right task.

In a *Forbes* article, George Bradt wrote: "There is an art to delegating involving discriminating between things you must 1) do well yourself, 2) do yourself, but just well enough, 3) delegate and supervise, 4) delegate without supervising, 5) do later, and 6) do never. By placing tasks in the latter five categories, you free up time to spend on the most important tasks in the first category."

As much as possible, you want to strive for clarity and consistency between the levels—especially when it comes to delegating with and without supervising. For example, I am responsible for my company's client satisfaction survey. It is a big project that's extremely important, so I personally manage it. But each year, I select a team to work with me. There are certain tasks that can be done without supervision, such as selecting the clients for the survey, (since this is based on agreed-upon criteria). Some aspects, such as drafting the analysis, are done with supervision, and others, such as developing and delivering the presentation, I handle with the team's input.

When you delegate, be explicit about whether you intend to delegate responsibility for the work while continuing to make the decisions, whether you intend to delegate responsibility for the work AND decisions, or whether you prefer a mix of the two (you are delegating responsibility for the work and the decisions, but you want to be kept informed).

Danielle learned a lot about delegation when she got her first promotion. As an assistant responsible for billing, she devised a great system for handling invoice payment. It was one of the reasons she advanced. But when the new assistant started making changes to the system, it irked Danielle. She had to remind herself, as long as the core function of the job was being done properly, she had to let the new assistant make the task her own. Danielle knew from me that if she didn't delegate the task, she wasn't going to have time for the new things she was being asked to do and her new assistant would not feel empowered.

Keep in mind even if your subordinate doesn't do a job quite as well as you, that's okay. I once had a boss who could legitimately do everyone's job better than them, but if he actually did he wouldn't have time to run the company! One of the hardest things I've had to do as a leader is let someone make a decision when I think they are making a mistake. Once I've delegated the authority for a decision, it's inappropriate and demotivating to override the decision even if I don't agree with it. Unless someone is about to put the business at risk, I just stay out of it.

For example, one of my directors wanted to hire a new employee. I felt fairly certain the candidate wasn't going to work out and did share my point of view, but I told the director it was his decision. He made the hire, and sure enough, it ended badly. However, the director learned what he needed from the experience and didn't make the same mistake again.

When I was promoted to the c-suite and was managing a senior group of executives, I realized it was time to establish formal "decision rights" so there wouldn't be confusion about who would make which decisions. Each of these leaders was running a department fairly autonomously, but there were also decisions that affected the enterprise. I drafted an extensive document that outlined all the decisions I could think of. We discussed and debated until we had a comprehensive list. For each item, we confirmed who would make the decision, who needed to be involved for input, and who needed to be informed. Here are the types of decisions we included:

- Organizational Structure changes.

- People: Hiring, firing, promotions, transfers, salary changes, and bonus allocations.
- Financial: Unbudgeted expenses outside of certain ranges, capital expenditures, etc.
- Sales/Contracts: Approvals for non-standard terms, discounts above targets, revenue or commission sharing, exceptions, etc.
- Product: Investment in new products or services, country expansion, changes to methodology or deliverables, shutting down a product or service.
- Marketing and Branding: Product naming, branding, changes to the website, etc.
- Mergers and Acquisitions (M&A) activity.

The time we spent developing this was well worth it. Everyone appreciated having input into the document, and there was no confusion going forward. And lately, we've adopted another more specific technique called RACI, otherwise known as RASCI.

DID YOU KNOW?

If you want employees to adopt a strategy and hold it close to their hearts, give them a pet! At least that's what eBay did in the mid-aughts. "RASCI the Decision-Making Mongoose" was the official mascot for a corporate policy at the online shopping mecca. The name RASCI is an acronym for the stakeholders in eBay's decision-making methodology. Here's what each of the letters stands for:

Responsible: The single decision maker, accountable for quality and timelines of process, agreements, relationships, deliverables, and decisions.

Approver: The individual to whom "R" is accountable in the decision-making process and who has the final sign-off.

Supporter: Implements the decision, accountable to "R" for agreed-upon work, timeframe, deliverables, and/or resources.

Consultant: Provides substantive input and sought by "R" during the decision-making before the actions are taken and plans are finalized.

Informed: Receives notice of the outcome after the decision is made.

If you were one of the eBay employees who received a plush RASCI toy in 2004 so that you'd remember to use the methodology every time you cuddled it in your cubicle, you're a part of history. RASCI is now used around the world to help leaders ensure accountability.

COPING WITH CHALLENGING LEADERSHIP SCENARIOS

Sometimes you get inspiration from strange places. I like to watch television, but since I don't have much time to do it, I check out my favorite shows while I'm working out. Once, when I was out of shows to watch, a co-worker suggested I download *Battlestar Galactica.* One evening while I was in Miami for a company meeting, I got some terrible news about a possible customer defection that would put a major business of ours in jeopardy. I was distraught.

The next morning, while on the treadmill watching my download, there was a disaster on the battleship show. The senior leader, Admiral Adama, was out of commission and the next in command, his son, Lee, had to step up and handle the situation. Lee was nervous but he did what was needed—he stayed calm, evaluated his options, pulled his team together, built consensus, and made the hard decisions.

Of course, in the end, they were all okay, and Lee was heralded by the crew and his father. The Cylons didn't exterminate the human race after all. I was inspired! I related to Lee as I also had a major problem to solve. Laugh if you like, but the episode motivated me to face my issue head on and marshal my resources to solve it.

While all the meeting's attendees had free time in the afternoon, I convened my leadership team. I wanted to let them know I was in it with them and we would all rally. I announced: "We've gotten some bad news, but let's keep it in perspective. We are smart, we know our business, and we are going to put our heads together and come up with a plan. But since we are in Miami and it's a beautiful day, let's not hole up in a conference room. Let's meet down by the beach."

When we got together, I reiterated I had confidence in my team's knowledge and expertise, and together we were going to do the best we could. That's all anyone could ask. "The sun is shining, no one is dead, and we'll figure it out," I told them. We did come up with a plan, and while the situation wasn't resolved in a 60-minute episode, in the end it all worked out.

Words of Wisdom

"Commit to yourself to courageously try new things, develop new skills, and ask for feedback early and often. Pause and capture your accomplishments, and measure and communicate about what you've discovered and learned."

—Gayle Fuguitt, chief, Customer Insight and Innovation, Foursquare.

MAKING TOUGH CALLS AND COMPLEX DECISIONS

Recently, I was working on a major transformation effort, and it was important we moved fast. My motto was "go, learn, iterate," which is the opposite of the old adage "measure twice, cut once." While both have their place, a leader must know when deciding things quickly is more important than being precise, and when precision takes precedence over speed. When making tough calls, I generally adhere to this process:

1. Outline all the possible options, even those I don't like. There are usually 3-5 options.
2. Gather information/data.
3. Lay out the pros and cons of the options.
4. Solicit opinions from others involved.
5. Make the call.

The length of time and the amount of effort expended at each stage depends on the importance of the decision and the weighting of speed versus precision. Sometimes, I can run through all of these steps in my head and be done. Other times, it might take longer to get to a point where I feel confident enough to act.

I have to accept that, occasionally, I will make the wrong call. But, as a leader, it is critical I take action in a timely manner. I will never have all the data, complete consensus, or a crystal ball. I need to just make the best decision I can with the information I have at the time. One of my husband's favorite expressions is: "Perfection is the enemy of good." Sometimes, getting from 90 percent to 100 percent isn't worth it in terms of lost time or additional cost.

Here's an example of how my process helped me decide whether to shut down a business. Several clients had cancelled a certain service, and we didn't know if we should discontinue offering it or continue to provide it. I first outlined all the options:

1. Do nothing (this is an option to remember, and, while it's often not attractive, it is worth mentioning). In this case, do nothing was to continue the service as it was.
2. Shut down the service.
3. Modify the service.

Next, I gathered information/data. How many clients were buying the service, how happy were they, and how much revenue did it generate? Was the service profitable?

I jotted down the pros and cons and solicited feedback from my colleagues. I uncovered a few interesting pieces of information along the way. While the service was profitable and the remaining clients were generally happy, there was a problem I didn't anticipate: Joe, a critical company resource, was spending an inordinate amount of time on the service, taking away from more important initiatives. This was certainly a disadvantage to continuing the service. However, I also learned a huge client who buys many services from us would be very unhappy if we discontinued this particular one. This was a negative to shutting it down.

So, with the scales virtually balanced, we turned to option three: modify the service. The team came up with an approach that would reduce the frequency of the service from monthly to quarterly. This would result in lower profits, but it would allow us to decrease the burden on Joe while still providing clients with enough value to keep them satisfied.

MEASURING SUCCESS

There are some things, like financial objectives and operational efficiencies, which can and should be measured. I value client and employee satisfaction surveys and use them as inputs to staffing and planning. These surveys not only help the leadership team, but they also help employees. Recall my early manager review scores forced me to face whether I wanted to be a manager or not, and this was life-changing for me.

Having said that, not everything worthwhile can be assessed via a metric or scorecard. Many leaders look to ROI analysis when making investment decisions to ensure there is a payout. Often too, a leader must focus on the big picture. I regularly ask myself: What is our long-term vision for the company? How can I make this a shared vision with my team? What extraordinary things do we want to accomplish to achieve our vision? How can I help motivate people to want to contribute? What changes to our culture do I need to encourage so employees are motivated? How do we all share in the success of the company?

So, in addition to quantitative metrics, I rely on the answers to these questions to ensure we are on track. To me, the ultimate measure of success is that our company is healthy and growing and our employees share in our vision, are engaged in pursuit of that vision, and feel ownership for achieving it.

RONI: THE RISK OF NOT INVESTING

There was a time, said the Business Learning Institute's Bill Sheridan, when doing nothing wouldn't cost you anything.

A hot new trend would emerge, and what would we do? Study it to death or try to master it before we took action on anything. Or better yet, let someone else do the hard work of building the blueprint so we could follow it later on without any risk.

We could get away with inaction because there was no sense of urgency. Things weren't changing all that quickly and we didn't have a million different competitors breathing down our necks. We were making money doing what we had always done. There was no point getting stressed over new stuff because we didn't have to.

Today, that kind of lethargy will kill you.

Sheridan commented that we spend too much time worrying about ROI (return on investment) and not nearly enough time focused on what Reggie Henry, the tech guru at the American Society of Association Executives, calls "RONI." RONI stands for "risk of not investing."

Given the speed in which things move today, RONI can be astronomical. The desire to wait to make a decision until a development is more certain can even be fatal to your career or your organization. Doing nothing is no longer the safe option and it will only cause you to fall further and further behind.

SURVEY SAYS: LEADERSHIP TRAITS THAT PROPEL AND DERAIL

According to DDI's global study of 15,000 executives in 18 countries, there are certain personality traits and attributes that make it more and less likely a person will succeed in a 21st century business world leadership role.

One section of the DDI report looked at hard-to-develop, positive traits (enablers) that grease leader success, and dysfunctional traits (derailers) that tend to trip them up. DDI examined these across three leader levels—strategic executive, operational, and mid-level. At each successive level, enablers are: exhibit stronger ambition and resilience and interpersonal sensitivity. Although the highest-ranking executives are generally less vulnerable to them, the list of derailers was a bit longer and included these traits:

- **Volatility**: displayed as inconsistency, distractibility, and moodiness. This trait threatens credibility for building trust through predictable actions and consistent follow-through.
- **Avoidant**: often seen as passive-aggressive conflict resolution, which poisons opportunities to influence and interact.
- **Perfectionism**: the need to micromanage work or delay decisions in pursuit of a 100 percent outcome.
- **Approval Dependent**: being ruled by the need for personal reinforcement and pleasing others.
- **Arrogance**: expressed as self-importance or insensitivity, the need to oversell their own importance, or influence others through intimidation.

- **Risk Aversion**: an unwillingness to make bold moves to drive the business forward.
- **Attention Seeking:** the desire to take center stage risks overshadowing those whose hearts they need the most. This lack of humility compromises trust.

Additionally, by profiling 243 CEO finalists in 48 organizations and benchmarking them against a larger database of leaders, DDI showed leaders who are successful enough to be considered for a CEO position are unlike other high performers. In terms of what they do to excel, CEO candidates more often obsess over execution and results, instantly and accurately size up complex business situations, and fixate on customer needs. CEO candidates are more likely to be intensely competitive, craving of attention, and either creative OR pragmatic. One especially intriguing finding? Twenty-one percent of CEO candidates are creative, conceptual strategists, and 29 percent are practical, no-nonsense operators, but only eight percent effectively balance both.

The research also examined where CEO candidates tend to struggle. Their top Achilles heel involves defaulting to the short-term. The so-called strategic plans these leaders make are often not very strategic at all. They solve operational dilemmas, but few generate effective, long-range growth strategies, so meaningful organizational change is rare.

Unfortunately, CEO candidates often treat talent as an afterthought. Their most rigorous planning seldom focuses on talent. Coaching is diplomatic but is often not goal-oriented, while talent development is perfunctory rather than strategic. And finally, they have trouble coming across as truly inspirational. When trying to rally the organization behind their plans, most leaders turn reflexively to financial projections even though it's more effective to lead from the heart. Sounds like what we've been saying all along!

CHAPTER SUMMARY

- Although leadership may involve management, the role of a leader is fundamentally different than that of a manager, and leaders will inevitably have different responsibilities than the ones they held in the past.
- A good leader inspires people to believe in the organization's strategy and want to be a part of it. They communicate what the vision means for the company, its clients, and its employees, as well as how individuals can contribute to making the vision a reality.
- Embracing different perspectives makes for a much richer discussion and better ultimate outcome. As tempting as it is to want to work with someone who thinks just like you, it is not nearly as productive as having a variety of points of view on your team.
- Effective delegating involves discriminating between things you must 1) do well yourself, 2) do yourself, but just well enough, 3) delegate and supervise, 4) delegate without supervising, 5) do later, and 6) do never. By placing tasks in the latter five categories, you free up time for important tasks in the first category.
- As a leader, it's critical to make important decisions in a timely manner. You will never have all the data, complete consensus, or a crystal ball. You just need to make the best decision you can with the information you have at the time.

- There are some things, like financial objectives and operational efficiencies, which can and should be measured. But not everything worthwhile can be assessed via a metric or scorecard. The ultimate measure of success may simply be: is your organization healthy and growing, and are your people engaged?

CHAPTER NINE

THE CAREER JOURNEY: WHERE TO NEXT?

When I was in second grade, I had the most wonderful teacher in the whole world. She was beautiful and nice and had perfect handwriting. The only things wrong with her were that she had a terrible last name (Miss Grassenflug) and at 24 she wasn't married, which was a crime to my seven-year-old friends and me. Since she was our idol, we couldn't imagine why she didn't have a husband to take care of her and help her change that silly last name (can you believe how backwards things were in the early '60s?). Nevertheless, from then on, I wanted to be a second-grade teacher.

Growing up, I only knew about certain careers: doctor, lawyer and yes, the more traditional female ones such as nurse, teacher, and flight attendant. I didn't have any role models in business. All my mothers' friends were stay-at-home moms, except one who was a teacher. So, teacher it was.

My father challenged me: "Honey, you are smart and you have good grades, why don't you become a doctor or lawyer?" But, these didn't appeal to me and, since I am extremely goal-oriented, once I had made up my mind, I stuck hard and fast to this goal for the next dozen years of my life.

I graduated high school a year early, at 17. I will admit I'd led a sheltered life and was pretty immature. My father insisted I stay home for the first couple of years of college, and then I could go anywhere I wanted. After two years at a local community college, I chose the University of Massachusetts because Massachusetts was known for its progressive education programs.

While I was gratified by my progress to become a teacher, I will confess during my full-time student teaching internship in my last year of college, I heard a small nagging voice in my head that said: "Uh oh, are you sure you want to do this every day, all day?" The truth was, I wasn't.

When I graduated from college in 1978, there were simply no teaching jobs, which, as it turned out, was a blessing in disguise. Originally, I thought I'd go back to school for a master's degree in education, but in the meantime, I did what everyone did back then. I turned to the newspaper classified ads to look for a job.

I answered an ad that said: "Work with computers, interesting work, no typing necessary." This was before PCs, so computers took up a whole room! This job involved filing computer tapes, which did not appeal to me and wouldn't work well with my long, 1970s fingernails. When I told Karl (the interviewer) that I wasn't interested, he mentioned another job as a "Gal Friday." Yes, there really was a job called "Gal Friday." This was a woman who provided a wide variety of clerical and administrative duties for an executive. It originated from Daniel Defoe's novel, *Robinson Crusoe*, in which the servant and constant companion was named Friday.

I explained, while I liked the company, given my college education I was overqualified for that job too, and had to pass. Throughout the whole process, I was professional and brought my "A" game to the interviews, even when I realized the jobs weren't for me. Because of this, Karl saw something in me, and on a hunch, he introduced me to the president of the company, Tom. Right on the spot, Tom offered me a job as a project director.

I said to Tom: "Hmm. Project director. That sounds interesting, but when I come into work and sit down at my desk, what will I do?" Bless his heart, he said: "Don't worry. We'll teach you." And that was how my career in market research began.

Sometimes you just have to start traveling down a road without necessarily knowing where you are going. I'm obviously in a very different place today, but I value every twist and turn my career has taken. We are never sure exactly where we'll end up, but there are certain principles we can follow to make sure we're proud and satisfied along the journey.

BE TENACIOUS AND RESILIENT

I recently had lunch with a business colleague who shared a story about her daughter Caylee and the power of tenacity and resilience. Caylee, a young and supremely hopeful young woman, applied to 12 colleges and was accepted to all except her first choice, X University.

Unfortunately, Caylee was obsessed with X University. The school had been voted one of the most beautiful campuses in America and was an up and coming, competitive university in terms of its academic and study abroad programs. Caylee knew from the minute she stepped on campus this was the school for her. She applied early and on decision day, woke up at midnight to see if she was accepted.

Caylee burst into tears when she read the word "DEFERRED." In her 18-year-old mind, "DEFERRED" meant "NO." Her mom sat on the edge of the bed, wiped a tear away from Caylee's face, and told her: "If you want something and believe you can achieve it, you need to be extra resilient and tenacious." Caylee looked at her mother and questioned the advice, thinking X University had made up its mind and that was that. But being reminded "deferred" didn't mean "not accepted" was one of the most important lessons in Caylee's life. The door was still open.

Caylee's mom encouraged her to keep plugging away and have the best academic semester of her high school tenure (just at the time when others were slipping into "Senior Slump"). She also recommended her daughter send X University a note reiterating her interest and sharing why the school was her first choice. Caylee kicked into high gear, sending X University updates about her grades, writing two extra essays, and informing the admissions team when she received a Creative Book Award for an AP Photography project. She set up a LinkedIn account and connected with one of X University's counselors.

Caylee didn't stop there. Then, she asked for extra references from her high school teachers, asked a girl she knew attending X University and her soccer coach to write letters on her behalf, and asked neighbors who knew someone in admissions to pen letters of recommendation. In short, Caylee did everything she could possibly do to gain acceptance to this college. X University had only 1,800 spots to offer to 10 times the number of applicants, but Caylee was moved from "DEFERRED" to "WAITLIST" and then finally to "ACCEPTED!"

On move in day, Caylee received an impromptu visit from X University's regional admissions counselor. She told Caylee her application, passion to attend, and tenacity throughout the process stood out among the 18,000 candidates who applied. Caylee's willingness to go after what she wanted in this situation literally changed and defined her life for the next four years.

Resilience will serve you well throughout your career. Randy Pausch was a professor at Carnegie Melon University who wrote a book called *The Last Lecture*. Before Randy died of pancreatic cancer, I had the chance to work with him. One of the many things I took from Randy was his attitude about brick walls. "The brick walls are there for a reason," he said. "The brick walls are not there to keep us out. The brick walls are there to give us a chance to show how badly we want something. The brick walls are there to stop the people who don't want it badly enough."

I don't like taking no for an answer and have applied this advice in my career as well. When I was in sales, I didn't give up until I was sure we couldn't offer the prospect something helpful. I tried multiple times, using different tactics and stopping just short of being annoying. When my current company launched a new service that tracked footwear, for instance, clients were initially skeptical. I quoted the president of a men's shoe company $70,000 for an annual subscription, and he told me I had "two too many zeros on the number!" We missed our budget in the first year of the service, but went on to exceed expectations in the second year. It simply took the tenacity to stick with it, and after a couple of years even the men's shoe "hold out" ended up coming onboard.

Growing up, one of my role models was Mary Tyler Moore. I later learned she almost didn't interview for the *Dick Van Dyke*

Show because she had lost three roles within two weeks and didn't want to risk another rejection. Her friend told her she should stop feeling sorry for herself and go on the interview. The rest is history. Mary's tenaciousness paid off, and yours will too.

Words of Wisdom

> *"Plan your career to be a lifelong journey that will scale multiple industries. Strategically use the first years of work to gain diverse experience and expand your skill set. Once you have mastered something, don't be afraid to move on."*
>
> *—Pam Salkovitz, former CEO, Nine West.*

TAKE RISKS

Similarly, you sometimes need to get out of your comfort zone and take risks or you may be left behind. It can be scary and no one likes to fail, but if you don't put yourself out there and try, you will never know. If I hadn't told Karl I felt overqualified for the "Gal Friday" position, I might never have gotten my first job as a project director.

In sixth grade, Danielle announced she was running for class president. She had a lot of great ideas and a fair amount of support, but anyone who has been to middle school knows these elections tend to be popularity contests.

I admired her passion and didn't want the experience to discourage her or dampen her confidence and enthusiasm. I told her I was very proud she was willing to take this risk and that she had little to lose. If she won the election, she would be class president, but if she didn't, she would have a notch on her belt from an experience few others had.

I suggested we have a get together with a dozen of her friends, win or lose. Danielle didn't win the election, but to this day, she remembers the experience with fondness rather than disappointment. And as she progresses in her career, Danielle always puts herself forward for new opportunities and asks for what she wants. Even if it doesn't work out, she learned at an early age she'll land on her feet.

RISE ABOVE YOUR PEERS

As you embark upon your work life, you will learn things they don't teach you in college. Your career will take paths you don't always expect and sometimes these will surprise you and make you a bit uncomfortable. Danielle was ecstatic to land her first job right out of college, but the euphoria didn't last. She noticed there was a clique among her co-workers—a group of people who ordered lunch together and went out for Happy Hour drinks. At first, Danielle figured she wasn't invited because she was new, and once they got to know her, she'd be included. But after several months, she still couldn't break through to the inner circle. She was frustrated, so she turned to me for advice.

"Work isn't high school," I told her simply.

Cliques exist in all walks of life, but they are exacerbated in school settings because kids progress from grade to grade together, with the older ones always remaining senior to the younger ones. But the work world is different. Two people who start on the same day in the same role can have wildly different paths. One can become the other's boss someday. I reminded Danielle that she had many other friends and at work, it was less important to be popular than it was to be successful. In an organization, unlike in high school, hard work, smarts, and dedication can put you ahead.

Less than a year into that job, Danielle's manager left and she was promoted into his role. Since the team was short-staffed, she took on extra work and people began to rely on her. Combine that with a boss they all didn't care for, and the team bonded over a common enemy. The clique saw Danielle in a different light and, finally, she started to feel like she fit in. The funny thing is, by the time that happened, she was on her way to a leadership role and didn't care as much. Danielle had learned there is a difference between being friends and being friendly, and this is an important distinction as you move up the ladder.

BEFRIEND HR

No matter what your role is now and where you would like to go in the near and far future, if your company has a Human Resources (HR) department, group, business partner, or person responsible for optimizing talent, you should take advantage of that fact. Reach out and meet your HR representative. Let them know you are excited about your current role, but also that you want a long-term career with the company. Assure them you are willing to work hard and do what is necessary to advance.

Your HR rep can be a great advocate. HR, after all, was instrumental in helping me find the sales management course I took early in my career, as well as the presidents conference I attended when I was promoted to lead a business unit. In addition to identifying training courses that might be appropriate to learn new skills, HR reps can help you scout out opportunities to volunteer for extracurricular activities, introduce you to people of influence, and serve as a sounding board if you run into difficulties.

I have many examples of the power of HR. Years ago, while talking with the HR team, I learned my company didn't have a very comprehensive onboarding program. I offered to lead a group to develop one, which gave me exposure to senior people and got me noticed. Also, HR once helped me save a valued employee. When I ran our Beauty group, I hired a talented young man right out of college. I was so enamored with the industry I didn't understand not everyone feels the same way! After about a year, this young man confidentially approached HR to say he loved the company and liked the work, but he wasn't connecting with fragrances and makeup. Shortly after, there was an opening in our video game business for which he was perfect. I lost a team member, but the company retained a key talent.

The bottom line? HR can assist in ways you cannot imagine yet! So, once you've made an initial connection, ask your rep if you can touch base every few months to share your progress, get feedback, and discuss any issues.

Words of Wisdom

"Always make sure it is in writing how your performance will be evaluated and measured. Ask for performance updates quarterly as it is critical to have clear direction on expectations so at the end of the year there are no surprises!"

—Katy Giffault, vice president,
Global Consumer Insights, Hasbro, Inc.

VALUE YOURSELF

I attended a Women's Foodservice Conference in Phoenix in which Victoria Medvec, the executive director of Northwestern

Kellogg's Center for Executive Management, was the keynote speaker. She told a story about women versus men and self-confidence. She said: "Let's pretend that the only criterion for becoming the CEO of a company is that you have to be able to breastfeed. The men interested in the position would still raise their hands for the job. They would say things like: 'While I can't actually breastfeed, my wife and I have four kids and I've watched her do it, so I would be able to do this job,' or: 'While I haven't done it myself, I am a quick study and I'm sure I could learn,' and so on. On the other hand, the interested women would wonder if their anatomy was good enough, would question their ability, and would generally hesitate to apply for the job. What's wrong with this picture?"

"Imposter Syndrome" is a term coined in 1978 by clinical psychologists Pauline Clance and Suzanne Imes. It refers to high-achieving individuals who can't internalize their accomplishments and persistently fear being exposed as a fraud. The first time I heard the term, I thought, is this actually a thing? Are there other people who feel this way too? Since I accidentally fell into my career in business and never imagined myself in an executive role, I sometimes worried I didn't belong. How could an elementary education major who never took a business course in college be trusted to run a multi-million dollar business? What if someone found me out? What if they learned I actually preferred reading *People Magazine* to the *Wall Street Journal*?

I started mentioning this syndrome to other senior people (mostly women) and was shocked to learn many of them shared the same concerns! These were very successful women running large businesses. It was unfathomable they would be the slightest bit insecure, and yet they were.

About 20 years ago, I was running a small business unit. It might have been my favorite job of all time. I related to the industries we tracked, I enjoyed the clients, I loved my team, and we were very successful. We had the highest revenue growth, the highest profit growth, the best client satisfaction, and the best employee satisfaction. What could be better?

Then, my boss got a new job and his role managing all the U.S. business units was available. The CEO called me into his office and offered me the job. This would be a promotion and a much bigger role. It also meant managing my peers, including one who had previously been my manager. I was not expecting this at all! I was happy in my current job and wasn't sure I was qualified for the bigger job, so my initial reaction was to say no. That certainly took him by surprise. Being a smart manager, he suggested I go home and think about it. I was so conflicted I cried the whole drive home.

My husband and I spent the evening discussing it. "You can do this—you know you can," Brad said. But I still wasn't convinced. Finally, he said something that made the decision clear. "Kar, you realize that if you don't take this job, someone else will." I did some soul searching and tried to be objective. I concluded, based on the success of my business unit, I really was the best candidate for the job.

Call it undervaluing myself or call it Imposter Syndrome, but it felt strange to admit I was the most deserving of the position. I'd come to believe it is impolite to say you're more qualified than someone else.

How did I get through it? Well, I thought back to the time I moved from being an individual salesperson to a sales manager and was able to make a bigger contribution. I decided if I could help share what made our business unit successful, then perhaps all the company's businesses could be more successful. I walked in the next day and accepted the job.

I'm often asked how to make the transition from peer to manager. I took my colleagues—now direct reports—aside one at a time. "I respect you for all that you do and look forward to continuing to work together," I told them. I didn't apologize or explain or come across as bossy and entitled, but in presenting plans proactively, I did demonstrate I understood my own value. During the ensuing months, I did everything I could to be a good manager and was sincere about wanting things to work out, but they had to meet me halfway.

Danielle has also been in the position of managing former peers. Her advice is to make sure your boss openly supports your promotion and clearly states the new rules of the game, because you don't want anyone to subtly or directly undermine you. Then, once in the position, lead with everything you've got. Yes, there is a risk one of your former colleagues might quit because you're now their boss, but hopefully the majority will embrace what you have to offer.

In my new role managing all the U.S. businesses, I kept reflecting on what I was good at and where I could add value. I decided I could help via strong communication up, down and across, and this became my mission. I told my team I would be their advocate for sending messages up to management, I would communicate down everything I heard about corporate objectives and happenings, and I would create forums and opportunities for dialoguing across so we could all share and learn from each other.

Overcoming Impostor Syndrome is not easy. These tips will hopefully help you gain confidence even if you haven't yet been promoted and reached an "official" senior level:

- Track your accomplishments and look at the list often (more on this coming up).
- Don't compare yourself to others. Set goals for what you want to do and focus on achieving those things.
- Do an honest evaluation of your strengths and weaknesses. While everyone focuses on fixing the weaknesses, also focus on building up and honing your strengths.
- Find people who believe in you both personally and professionally and reach out to them for support.
- When you receive a compliment, don't negate it or deny it. Simply say, "thank you."
- Focus on helping others instead of yourself. As C.S. Lewis said: "Humility is not thinking less of yourself, it is thinking of yourself less."
- Talk with people you respect to see if they share similar concerns. Work together to overcome them. Remember, even brilliant and famous people occasionally admit to feeling like frauds. Try to laugh about it.

It is not attractive to brag, but there are times when you need to make sure your boss or others know what you have accomplished. While HR and your managers should help facilitate your growth, your career is ultimately your responsibility.

Someone who is strong and confident generally wants to work with other high performers. They want to be on an A team. This is why, as an A player, you must document your achievements.

Start a file today. If you get an email from a colleague or a client thanking you or complimenting something you've done, add it to the file. If you've been given specific goals or objectives, keep them handy and work the list—ensuring you are addressing everything on it. If you need help to accomplish a specific goal, ask. For example, if your boss said you need to hone your presentation skills but you haven't had a chance to present anything, see if there is an assignment that will afford you the opportunity. It's fine to reference your objective and the desire to accomplish it.

Danielle has taken this a step further. She looks at the job requirements for the next level up and works that list too. It's much easier to ask for a promotion if you have achieved everything on your list and are already operating at the next level.

A few notes of caution. Your file of accomplishments should be long and comprehensive, but don't ever do a data dump on your manager. Choose examples from the file that demonstrate your mastery of a specific task or skill. These examples can also be used when meeting with a senior person or a new manager who needs to know what you have been working on.

What if you have achieved all the criteria for your level but are denied a promotion? Make sure you understand the reasons. Are there softer skills you are missing, such as communicating tactfully or being assertive in meetings? Ask for specific examples of what you need that you are not currently demonstrating. If nothing is missing, inquire about what is holding you back. A lack of positions at the next level is sometimes a legitimate issue. In this case, ask about the possible timeline for an opening.

This is also where your friend in HR can come in handy. They can look beyond your current department for appropriate openings at the next level elsewhere in the company. If none are forthcoming, it might be time to look for a new organization.

My friend's daughter, Monica, ran into a frustrating situation. Monica is a go getter. She's ambitious but also willing to put in the necessary work to get ahead. She followed my advice and kept track of her accomplishments. She had a file full of client compliments. Additionally, Monica was maniacal about achieving the objectives for her level. During her review discussion, she was told she couldn't be promoted because she needed to be in her current role for at least two years. "What does time have to do with it?" she asked. "I've clearly mastered the skills at my level and many at the next level too."

"It's out of my hands," said her boss. Monica was too angry to pursue it further and found a higher-level position at another company. Upon hearing she was leaving, her boss's boss and the head of HR tried to get her to stay.

Monica felt it was too little, too late. "If you want to hold onto your strong performers, you need to stop thinking of career progression on a timeline and focus on the person and their accomplishments," she told them. "I had to do what was right for me and my career."

Words of Wisdom

"If you desire to keep moving up in an organization and/or change career paths, seek out stretch assignments that allow you to build out your network with purpose (beyond your current responsibilities and potentially with other departments). And always, always, always exceed job performance expectations in your current role (even if it is just a stepping stone position)."

—Kim Cupelli, vice president, Tyson Foods.

OPERATE ABOVE AND BEYOND

Let's say there's a job you really want. Hopefully, you now realize nothing should stop you! I recently talked with Heather, a young woman who is a great networker. She had met an executive from a well-known media company at a conference and they hit it off. He said he would love to have her work at his firm someday. She told him she was happy in her current role, but they should keep in touch.

Several months later, the exec reached out to Heather about a vice president position. She interviewed with the chief marketing officer, who informed her the position in question would be reporting to an SVP. However, that SVP role had not yet been filled. So, Heather sent the CMO a note saying: "I don't mean to be presumptuous, but might I throw my hat in the ring for the SVP position? I am a VP at my current firm, overseeing a cross-functional team of over 100 people and leading the largest P&L in our division, so I know I could bring a lot to the table in this type of leadership position."

Heather may or may not get the SVP position, but simply having the courage to put herself out there gives her a much better shot. As long as you are professional and armed with evidence of your value, you have little to lose and a lot to gain!

Setting yourself apart from the crowd is particularly important when you are first starting out or new to a company. Of course, you need to do the basics such as showing up on time, being prepared, working hard, and doing your job well. But how do you demonstrate that you're one to watch?

My strategy for standing out has always involved volunteering. In one instance, my company had been doing pricing in an ad hoc way and wanted a more professional approach via an official pricing manual. I didn't know anything about writing a pricing manual, but I offered to do it. Little did I know that volunteering to author the pricing manual would be a turning point in my career. A short time after completing the document, there was an opening for a sales manager. Several of us were equally successful at selling, but because of the visibility I'd acquired thanks to the pricing manual, I was the one selected. This promotion jump-started my career as a manager.

I've historically volunteered for anything and everything I could, and not just specific to my job responsibilities. If there was a task force or a committee that needed help, I raised my hand. I joined a committee to determine how two divisions might collaborate better, and, as I mentioned earlier, I helped lead a task force for onboarding new employees.

Volunteering has been a great way for me to learn new things, meet a broader group of people, and increase my exposure. In fact, years later, when I had kids and joined the PTA, I found myself volunteering for things all the time. I finally had to force myself to sit on my hands so that I wouldn't take on more than I could handle while working full-time!

What if your company doesn't have committees or task forces for you to join? See if you can create one. Identify something that needs improvement and lead a group to provide recommendations. Start a business book club. Be a buddy for a new hire. If you attend a training class or a business event or conference, summarize the learnings and share them with your team. Or, organize a "Lunch 'n Learn" on a topic with which you have some experience.

I was impressed recently by two young women in one of our regional offices. They proactively started a young professionals group, organizing opportunities to get together and discuss a topic and socialize. They even invited me to their office to lead a discussion on leadership. What a smart way to get my attention!

There are other ways to take initiative besides leading or joining committees and groups. When I was in sales, I launched a *Sales Tip of the Week* program. I gave everyone an empty binder labeled "Sales Tips." I gathered tips from my peers and sent a page around each week until the book was filled with tips (this was before email). As a modern twist on this, Danielle started a "Friday Funday" email. Each Friday, she collected relevant industry articles and links and sent them in a single email to a targeted distribution list. People began forwarding the email, and before long, others requested to be added. Within a short period of time, the distribution had grown to well over a hundred people, including the company executives. Danielle had created her own brand! When an opportunity came up to be part of a new business pitch or special assignment, Danielle was tapped because she had demonstrated business knowledge, was proactive, and was known by senior leadership.

One caveat about volunteering and taking initiative: remember that it needs to be above and beyond your regular job and shouldn't detract from your core responsibilities. If you don't have the bandwidth to do it all well, it's better to pass than to under-deliver.

Another part of operating above and beyond is going out of your way to meet senior-level individuals, which we talked about earlier. When I was 21-years-old and I took the job as a project director, I did a bold thing. Tom, the president, had hired me, but I had never met Marty, the owner of the company. It was a small firm at the time, and I passed by Marty's big, fancy office every day when I came into work. One day I just walked in and said: "Hello. I wanted to stop in and introduce myself. I'm Karyn Schoenbart, and I'm new here. It's very nice to meet you." I put out my hand for him to shake. I don't recall what Marty said next, but years later, he commented that he always remembered my courage.

Today, I suggest a subtler approach. Let's say the CEO or division president spoke at a company or external event that you attended. You could send them an email about the talk, trying to be as specific as possible. For example, instead of: "I enjoyed your speech," you could say: "I was inspired by your comments about how we need to be more external in our approach. Since I service the ABC account, I am going to visit more clients in-person this quarter." If you are compelling enough, you might get a response and an opportunity to reconnect. If the executive asks you to keep them posted, be sure to follow up.

Once you have established rapport, take it a step further and ask for an in-person connection. Your ability to make this happen may depend on logistics, but you could say something like: "The next time you are in town, I'd love the opportunity to talk with you more about ABC and perhaps get your advice on a few things." Most senior people are open to this type of dialogue, especially if it is genuine.

If you do get a meeting with a higher-up, be prepared. I hate it when I take the time to meet with someone, and they come in with a blank sheet of paper and no discussion items planned. Ideally, you want to get the senior person engaged and talking. Consider the following steps:

- Share something interesting or important you are working on, but keep it brief.

- Ask their opinion, advice, or a relevant business question (e.g. "you mentioned in the all-hands meeting we are expanding internationally. Can you share which countries you are thinking about and whether you might consider me for an international assignment?)
- Ask what you can do in your current position to help the company achieve its goals.
- If the executive is working on a special project or initiative, see if you can help.
- Ask if you can meet or connect sometime again in the future.
- Follow up with a thank you note.

Should you copy your current manager on these exchanges? It depends. Ideally, your manager is supportive and delighted you are getting exposure to an executive. Unfortunately, this isn't always the case, so you need to use your best judgment. Sometimes it is better to ask for forgiveness than permission. If you are just reaching out to introduce yourself or make a comment about a talk you heard, you can probably do it without copying your manager. If you get a meeting, then it is appropriate to let your manager know and perhaps share your meeting agenda to get advice on topics that might be of interest to the executive.

Words of Wisdom

"Never be afraid to express interest in an opportunity that could inspire you."

—Lynnette Cooke, global CEO, Kantar Health.

DID YOU KNOW?

Many career journeys involve at least one major pivot, and most would agree such a move is both exciting and scary. It may help you to learn these immensely successful individuals were once doing something completely different, and many people don't get their "big breaks" until they are well into their 30s or 40s!

- Billionaire Amazon.com founder Jeff Bezos: Started as an investment banker.
- Homemaker extraordinaire Martha Stewart: Started as a Chanel model.
- Spanx founder Sara Blakely: Started as an office supply salesperson.
- Cooking phenomenon Julia Child: Started as a CIA intelligence officer.
- A list actor Harrison Ford: Started as a carpenter.
- Poet Allen Ginsberg: Started as a cargo ship worker.
- Singer Elvis Costello: Started as a computer programmer.
- Kentucky Fried Chicken founder Harland "Colonel" Sanders: Started as a gas station operator.
- Entertainment magnate Walt Disney: Started as a newspaper editor.
- Talk show host Ellen DeGeneres: Started as a paralegal.

WIELD THE POWER OF THE PEN

Another of my favorite ways to stand out is by offering to take notes. This can occur in a breakout group, a brainstorming session, a planning meeting, or nearly any situation where a group is convening. I've been known to grab a marker and start writing on the easel or white board. Maybe it was the teacher in me that got me started doing this, but I've discovered two things: 1) the person with the pen gets more control over the conversation and the content and 2) the very act of taking notes can demonstrate leadership.

I've used the note-taking strategy both inside and outside of work. For example, my husband and I own a small apartment in a beach community of 40 condominiums. The resident manager left, and we needed to hire a new one. Since this person would live on the property and have entry access to all apartments, getting the right individual was critical. My husband suggested I run for a board seat so I would be part of the interviewing team. "Kar, we really need the right person for this job," he said. "You are good at interviewing and assessing people. It will be really helpful to the community if you do this." How could I say no?

I was voted in and chose the position of secretary. As soon as I was appointed, my neighbor Betsy approached me. "Karyn, you don't know what you are getting yourself into," she warned. "A few years ago when I was on the board, I had a terrible experience. The board was comprised of a bunch of chauvinistic retired businessmen who didn't respect my opinion. They were condescending and only expected me to fetch them coffee. Good luck!"

Uh oh, I thought. My husband just laughed and said, "They have no idea what they're in for."

Before the first meeting occurred, I took charge. I sent the board a professionally-prepared agenda. Since these gatherings took place on the weekend at the beach, I indicated we should try to be as efficient as possible. The last thing anyone wants is to spend their time off in a meeting indoors. I recommended we start and end on time so we could get back out in the sun.

Being secretary and taking notes gave me control. I was respectful of the president and the other board members who were more experienced than I was, but I used the agenda to ensure we stayed on track. I often interjected with a summary of the talking points for the purpose of the minutes, and so we could keep the discussion moving. If we got stuck on a point for too long, I'd ask for a vote so we could resolve the issue and move on to the next topic. I used my role as secretary to make the meeting effective, and along the way, I earned the other board members' respect. I actually didn't find them chauvinistic at all. Some were opinionated and there were heated debates at times, but I was able to corral the discussions in a productive way because I had the power of the pen. We hired a great resident manager and, by the way, no one ever asked me to get them coffee.

SNAG MENTORS AND SPONSORS

You have probably heard the terms "mentor" and "sponsor" before, but what's the difference? Generally speaking, a mentor provides either formal or informal guidance for career decisions and can be placed anywhere inside or outside your organization. In my experience, mentoring relationships work best when they are organic rather than forced and when there is a natural and authentic chemistry between the mentor and mentee. Formal assigned mentoring relationships that require reporting back are too often a "check the box" process and not as productive. A sponsor, on the other hand, is a senior-level individual within the organization who, as your advocate, has the influence to increase your visibility and opportunities. While I have benefited from both, the sponsors in my life have pushed my career along further than mentors.

Mentors and sponsors serve different roles and both are important, but a Randstad U.S.A. blog post reported on an intriguing study conducted by Sylvia Ann Hewlett and her think tank, the Center for Talent Innovation. The research looked at 12,000 men and women in white collar jobs across Britain and the United States and found sponsorship beats mentorship when it comes to career progression—especially for women struggling to climb higher than middle management.

According to the study, when it came to asking for a pay raise, the majority of men (67 percent) and women (70 percent) resisted confronting their boss. However, with the backing of a sponsor at work, nearly half of men and 38 percent of women made the request. When it came to getting assigned to a high-visibility team or stretch assignment, 43 percent of male employees and 36 percent of females approached their managers and made the request. With a sponsor, however, the numbers rose to 56 percent and 44 percent, respectively. So, if you have to choose where to expend your energies, this research indicates identifying a strong sponsor should be first, followed by recruiting a few effective mentors.

Both sponsor and mentor relationships can be same-gender or cross-gender. Much has been said about the importance of women helping women, and I'm all for that. My mother was my first role model, and I had a female manager for many years who was a great mentor. But the men in my life have helped my career as well. Starting with my father, who taught me about profits versus revenue and that you need to value your product; to my first manager, Adam, who was patient in teaching me the basics; to the manager who allowed me time to get used to the concept of going to Europe; to the CEO who has pushed me through most of my career; to my husband who always supports me and shares his opinions and advice.

As a leader myself, I always encourage both male and female leaders to identify employees they believe in and then do everything they can to propel those talented individuals forward. By using the tips in this chapter to go above and beyond, stand out, and be that one to watch, you'll be one of those talented individuals!

Words of Wisdom

"Finding a mentor and identifying your sponsors is always sage advice. Based upon my own experience, I highly recommend getting involved in your industry associations early on. Volunteers are always welcome, and you will find yourself in the company of more experienced professionals, expanding your network while building your brand."

—Carol Campbell, founder and CEO,
Women in Consumer Technology.

LATERAL MOVES

Job advice site Monster.com recently discussed the concept of career metabolism. This is when you have stayed put in a job longer than your mind and body want you to, and it's time for a change. Regardless of whether it's a good time, overstaying your welcome in a position may result in emotional and/or physical turmoil.

If you aren't due for a promotion and your current role is not due to change in any significant way, you might consider a lateral move. A lateral move involves transitioning to another type of job at the same level, perhaps in a different group, department, or function.

Companies generally like lateral moves because it's a way to keep people they trust and who are already known to do good work. The lateral move strategy offers an antidote to the "I'm-dead-ended-and-bored" lament heard so often in organizations today. It also saves organizations substantial recruiting and training fees.

How do you know a lateral move is right for you? Monster.com provided the following clues:

- You want more challenge but not more responsibility, because your plate is already too full outside of work.
- Your spouse is being moved and your company has a facility in the same location.
- You and your boss/colleague have locked horns and there doesn't seem to be any way to fix the situation.
- The functions your unit performs are being outsourced, but you don't want to leave the company.
- You're taking courses or completing a degree and don't want the stress of a promotion at the moment.
- You're preparing for an eventual move and want to spend some time in a functional area where you haven't had that much experience.
- There's an opportunity to report to someone in another unit from whom you can learn a great deal.

Should one or more of these scenarios pertain to you, it's worth a conversation with your manager or HR representative. A lateral move could be just the thing you need to kick-start your career journey.

CONSIDER INDEPENDENCE

I have always worked for companies, but I recognize there is something appealing about a career journey that takes you off on your own. I talked with some entrepreneurial friends of mine in order to offer you some solid advice on this path.

Don was laid off from a large ad agency due to a merger. His clients said they would follow him wherever he landed, but Don found no other agency could offer him the same independence or compensation he enjoyed at his previous position. Meg started her own gig because she fell in love with someone well known in her industry and had trouble finding an employer who didn't perceive the relationship as a conflict of interest.

Lee is a licensed social worker who went into business for herself because she wanted more control over her income and lifestyle. Jan launched a company in retail apparel because she was dissatisfied with the way her employers handled financials and her workload, title, and compensation compared to her male counterparts. Once faced with the challenge, Don, Meg, Lee, and Jan each took a leap of faith and gave it a try.

I asked my friends what aspect of being an entrepreneur gives them the greatest satisfaction. For Don, there is joy in knowing every decision—for better or worse—is his to make and take responsibility for. He finds it liberating. Meg takes pride in the fact that she started her business from nothing. "Each year I've worried if I'd still be in business the following year, and it's now 21 years later," she said. "I also love starting a project with just ideas and having physical evidence of my influence at the end."

Lee feels her business allows her to pursue her passion. "I love working with patients to have them better understand themselves and make strides to get what they want for their lives," she commented. For Jan, success is the greatest reward. "I love knowing that what I've created is working, that it's making money for my customers and that I can share in the profit."

Of course, starting a business isn't as easy as it may sometimes appear. For Don, navigating the unsteady income has been a challenge. "Our clients' budgets can swing widely from month to month and year to year, so our income really varies even though our fixed costs like salaries and rent stay the same and actually tend to go up." Similarly, Meg has been daunted by the need to market constantly and the lack of a reliable work schedule. "Sometimes, I don't know when and where the next project is coming from," she said. "And then there's the other side of it, which is having too much work and needing to say no!" Lee cited the isolation of working for herself, while Jan mentioned slow periods in her business—even if they are predictable.

I asked my friends about the advice they'd give someone who is considering launching a new business. Don was pragmatic. "Make sure you have access to credit, a working relationship with a bank, and enough cash to get you through at least the first year." Meg also discussed money right off. "You need very deep pockets to carry yourself, so be prepared. I was fortunate that my current employer asked me to stay on as a consultant and actually became my first client. That's an ideal way to go." Lee said it's important to know your specialization and where you are going to get customers. "You need a network, a community from which you can get referrals," she suggested. "And also, be willing to get supervision and learn from others."

Jan shared starting a new business is often a gradual process.

"Start at a place you feel comfortable and grow from there," she said. "Find people you trust with whom you can work and share ideas, and then go for it!"

SURVEY SAYS: WHAT ARE THE KEYS TO EXECUTIVE SUCCESS?

An article by Link Gan and Alan Fritzler described a LinkedIn study of the career paths of nearly 500,000 site members who worked at a Top 10 consultancy between 1990 and 2010 and became a VP, CXO, or partner at a company with at least 200 employees. For the 64,000 individuals that reached this milestone, LinkedIn analyzed both observable and inferred traits from their profiles, including educational background, gender, work experience, and career transitions. All in all, the likelihood of becoming an executive is only about 17 percent, and LinkedIn wanted to uncover if specific activities or attributes boosted people's chances.

The research found individuals who worked across multiple job functions (for example, marketing, sales and finance) had a better understanding of the business operations needed to become an executive. Each additional job function provided a boost of three years of work experience. On the other hand, individuals who changed industries—perhaps because of the learning required or relationships lost—were not as effective at progressing up the ladder.

What about advanced degrees? The research showed for the average person in the sample, having an MBA from a top five program (per *U.S. News and World Report*) provided a net boost equivalent to 13 years of work experience. In contrast, a non-top ranked MBA offered a net boost of only five years. And while other advanced degrees such as a Ph.D., Juris Doctor, or non-business master's degree have increased in popularity, they didn't provide the same boost as an MBA.

Another study, featured in the GMAC *Corporate Recruiters Survey Report*, echoed LinkedIn's findings related to MBA benefits. In that survey, approximately 80 percent of responding companies said they were currently hiring recent MBA graduates into middle-management level positions, and nearly 60 percent said they were increasing the number of MBA hires from the previous year. The respondents commented they were attracted to newly-minted MBAs because of their skills in business and marketing analytics, communication, and problem solving.

LinkedIn found, in the U.S., working in New York City increased the chances of becoming an executive, while working in Houston and Washington, DC, decreased the chances. Internationally, Mumbai and Singapore provided the greatest boost, while Sao Paulo and Madrid had the most negative effects. LinkedIn speculated this could be in part due to the nature of the industries that are prevalent in these cities (for example, the financial services industry tends to be more hierarchical than the high-tech industry), as well as the higher concentration of company headquarters in those regions.

Interestingly, all of these factors have the same effect on both men and women's careers, although a woman with the same profile as a man needed an average of 3.5 more years of work experience to reach the same probability of becoming an executive.

CHAPTER SUMMARY

- Resilience will serve you well throughout your career. Brick walls are there for a reason. They are not there to keep us out, but rather to give us a chance to show how badly we want something.
- Sometimes, you need to get out of your comfort zone and take risks or you may be left behind. It can be scary and no one likes to fail, but if you don't put yourself out there and try, you will never know what might have happened.
- Gain an advantage by getting to know your HR representative. Let them know you are excited about your current role but also want a long-term career at the company. Assure them you are willing to work hard and do what is necessary to advance, including making a lateral move if appropriate.
- Volunteering is a terrific way to learn new things, meet a broader group of people, and increase your exposure. Join committees or task forces that will get you noticed, or identify something that needs improvement and lead a group to provide recommendations.
- If you are denied a promotion, make sure you understand the reasons. Are there skills you are missing? Ask for specific examples of what you need that you are not currently demonstrating. If nothing is missing, then inquire about what is holding you back.
- Offer to take notes. The person with the pen gets more control and the very act of taking notes can demonstrate

leadership. Assuming you do it well, people will view you as the leader since you are in a position to steer the conversation.

- A mentor provides either formal or informal guidance for career decisions and can be placed anywhere inside or outside your organization. A sponsor, on the other hand, is a senior-level individual within the organization who, as your advocate, has the influence to increase your visibility and opportunities. Both are advantageous in the right time and place.

CHAPTER TEN

THE BALANCING ACT: WHAT IT MEANS TO HAVE IT ALL

I DESPISE THE WORD "REGRET." I think its true definition should be "a complete waste of time and energy." That's not to say one shouldn't learn from mistakes, but learning is different than feeling sad or disappointed over something that happened. I try not to fester over things I could or should have done differently. Managing everything associated with working and raising a family is hard enough!

Of course, not everything in life works out perfectly. For example, I wish I could have taken advantage of the opportunity to get an MBA. My company offered to sponsor me, free of charge, to attend Columbia University's executive program. However, the timing would have required going to school in addition to working full time and raising two small children. Looking back, I would have made the same decision. To quote Oprah Winfrey: "You can have it all, but you can't have it all at once."

Both working women and working men today must consider what "having it all" really means. I feel lucky that over the last 30+ years, I have maintained a rewarding and satisfying career, brought up two terrific kids who are grown and have successful careers of their own, and partnered with a wonderful man in a long and happy marriage.

But there have been sacrifices. In addition to passing on the MBA, for long stretches of time I didn't exercise, barely read a newspaper, rarely watched TV except for kids' shows, and only hung out with the parents of my kids' friends. Once, I forgot to feed my kids dinner, and another time, I left them at religious school. But all in all, things have worked out okay. Here, I'll share stories and practical tips for how I balanced work, kids, and marriage with the hope something will either inspire you or at least make you laugh. I want to emphasize that while I'm a woman, my advice is directed to all working professionals because the decisions we must make in the service of balance are relevant for everyone.

My mother was a stay-at-home parent and was really good at it. She was the class mother who went on all the field trips and was always waiting for us when we got home from school. She even cooked my father, my brother, and me a hot breakfast every morning! Given my family background, I had a dilemma when I was pregnant for the first time. I loved my job and had just been promoted to vice president. I knew in my heart staying home all day wasn't for me, but I worried how my parents would react. I was grateful when they supported my decision.

Even though I wanted to work while raising my children, I was committed to being the best mother I could be. I was lucky to have a great role model and knew firsthand what it felt like to have a good mother. My mom treated us with love and respect. She always listened and was open to hearing what was on our minds. She showed me the way, and I believed if I set my mind to it, I could be just as good a mother as she was, regardless of whether I was working full time or not.

THE MOMMY WARS

The concept of "Mommy Wars," or pitting working mothers against stay-at-home moms, started when my kids were little. I had no time for this nonsense. My best friend from high school, Rose, stayed at home with her children. I admired her tremendously, but never envied her life. Being home is hard! Rose cleaned her own house, washed all the laundry, cooked every meal, and did odd jobs too. For me, working full time made more sense, and for Rose, staying home did. It was as simple as that.

I was living in a suburban community in which most of the women didn't work. Working peers of mine said they felt they were being judged when they picked up their kids at school. As a result, they only befriended other working mothers. I didn't agree with this. While I couldn't socialize during the day, I went out of my way to be part of the community by joining the PTA, keeping up with playdates, and doing my fair share of carpooling on nights and weekends. I made friends with the moms I liked, regardless of their work status. I didn't look down on them for their choices and hoped they felt the same.

I strived to maintain a balanced perspective in my choice of reading material. *Working Woman* was first published in 1978, and in targeting employed women, was unlike the other women's magazines that covered either motherhood or fashion. But instead of just reading *Working Mother* magazine, which fed me stories that fit my worldview, I also read *Parents* to get unfiltered advice on parenting, helping me understand the joys and difficulties of raising children regardless of one's work status. Reading both of these forced me to make my own decisions on when to prioritize my career and when to prioritize my family.

DIVIDE, CONQUER, AND OUTSOURCE

In the 1950s, men generally went to work and made the money, and women stayed home to raise the family. Regardless of whether this was right or wrong, good or bad, at least it was clear. The roles were well-defined. In the modern world, roles are thankfully being re-established, but they are less cut and dry.

Sometimes, people who are happily married say their spouse is their best friend, and I describe my husband that way too. But in the context of this book, Brad is also my LBP (Life Business Partner). Living together, working two full time jobs, managing a household, and raising a family at the same time is not that different from trying to run a successful business. And just like in a business, you need to know who is going to do what. Brad and I have done a pretty good job with the divide and conquer dance. We focus on what we do well, or occasionally, on who hates the chore the least.

For example, when Danielle was born, we decided we would take turns waking up early on Saturdays and Sundays. Since my husband is not a morning person, I quickly realized having him get up early wasn't worth it. He was miserable the whole day, which in turn made me miserable. So, I took the morning shift and Brad reciprocated by dealing with nighttime issues.

I'll admit over the years, our chores often split along traditional gender roles. I was responsible for most of the things having to do with the kids, like arranging carpools and helping with homework, while Brad tended to care for household tasks like the yard, electronics, and house repairs. But it worked, and if it works, that's a good thing.

One of my colleagues is a senior vice president with three children. When I asked what she does for childcare, she explained her husband is a stay-at-home dad. "Did you plan it that way?" I asked. She laughed and said when her kids were little and the family relocated, she was making slightly more money than her husband so they decided she would take the new job and he would initially stay home. Eighteen years later, it's still working out just fine.

Often, both parties in a married couple work because it is hard to live on one income. Nevertheless, I recommend outsourcing as much as you can afford so you can spend more time doing the things you love with the people you love. If you like cooking, then by all means cook, but most people don't like laundry or cleaning. My colleague Diana, who recently had her second child, raved about grocery delivery services like Fresh Direct and Peapod that give her an hour of time back every weekend.

In my life, cooking is one area I try to outsource whenever possible. When I was single, my idea of dinner was cheese and crackers. If I was feeling especially industrious, I'd melt the cheese on the crackers in the microwave.

I'm actually a danger in the kitchen. One time, I almost set an entire apartment building on fire. I was making homemade chocolate chip cookies…ok, they were slice and bake. I lived in a pre-war apartment building and I had never used the oven before. In preparation for my big cookie bake, I turned on the oven to preheat it. After about a minute, I realized I was supposed to light the pilot light, so, match in hand, I approached the oven. POOF! I burned my hand and almost set my hair on fire. If I had waited a few minutes longer, I probably would have destroyed the building.

Today, if there is a party or event where bringing food is required, instead of worrying about it, I offer to bring the drinks or the paper goods. Sometimes, I'll even have my friend Rose make her famous noodle pudding on my behalf. I buy her a small gift or take her out to lunch to show my appreciation. It's okay, because by now, everyone knows cooking isn't my thing. I often repeat one of my favorite lines: "We can't all be good at everything." You can achieve better balance by focusing on what you are good at and finding a way to get the rest done with minimal grief.

Professional organizer Lisa Woodruff of Organize 365 shared some additional outsourcing ideas. "I have a repair list for my handyman and call him when I have a whole day's worth of work," she said. "Professional organizers can help with things like digital photo scanning and photo album creation, and Amazon is my go-to store for all of my shopping needs. Instead of putting something on a list to buy later, I just open my Amazon app, order it right away, and it's delivered to my doorstep within two days."

When faced with a bevy of time-consuming chores, paying for occasional assistance really will improve the quality of your life!

DID YOU KNOW?

If you thought work/life balance was a 21st century ideal, it may surprise you that it's actually one of the oldest labor-related constructs. Back in 350 B.C., Greek philosopher Aristotle wrote about it in his publication, *Nicomachean Ethics and Politics.* "The whole of life is divided into two parts, business and leisure, war and peace, and of actions some aim at what is necessary and useful, and some at what is honorable," he said. Leisure time, however, wasn't an equal opportunity endeavor. Aristotle believed in a society in which the majority of people worked so the upper-crust of society had more time to pursue intellectual and otherwise "honorable" interests. In his time, work (or ponos, which notably translates to "sorrow") was purely a means to an end—with that end being societal survival.

MUTUAL RESPECT AND PERSPECTIVE

Brad and I have made our crazy life work because we have mutual respect for each other and for our careers. He is proud of my accomplishments, and the feelings are mutual. Don't get me wrong, we've had our share of tough times. I recall the dreaded Sunday nights when we would wait with baited breath to see if the babysitter showed up before we had to start our work week, and the time we had to fire one for drinking on the job. I remember when a child woke up sick on a day when we both had jam-packed schedules. In these situations, Brad and I debated who could take off from work. But we didn't argue about whose career was more important. We are a team and in it together.

Over time, things balance out, but there have definitely been situations when one job takes precedence. When Brad is on call at the hospital, I know I have to step up and take care of most things since he is stressed out enough. When I'm on a long trip, particularly to Asia or Europe, he knows not to bother me with minor issues.

The toughest situation we've faced involved geography. Brad initially took a job on Long Island because I was doing well in my organization and had just been promoted. Additionally, we had family there, which made it a lot easier to raise children. But it wasn't Brad's ideal job, and after a few years, it didn't work out. I realized he needed to expand his search outside the area, which might mean leaving my position. In order to make an informed decision, we wrote out the pros and cons of moving. Given the cons vastly outweighed the pros, Brad was determined to and eventually did find a great position locally.

Mutual respect between partners is easier when you make an extra effort to give to the relationship. When our kids were small, my relationship with Brad did get shafted in terms of time. There were only so many hours in the day, and work and kids took priority. But we did regularly schedule date nights so the two of us could go out for dinner, sometimes alone and sometimes with another couple. The places we went usually weren't fancy since we had to pay for a babysitter, but it was a chance to reconnect and spend some time together. This was an important part of keeping our marriage alive and well in the midst of chaos.

Here's something else working parents often face: the need to balance allegiance with your spouse with your need to parent your children. This one is important at work too, especially with matrix management relationships. You don't want your children or your employees to pit you against each other. Brad and I developed a system for this, and always strived to show a united front. This is parenting 101, but it isn't as easy as it seems because we didn't always agree. He's a worrier and I'm more laissez-faire. We often fought in our bedroom behind closed doors about whether to let Danielle go away to a horse show or allow Eric to travel cross-country alone for a debate tournament.

Since I'm the better communicator, it was my job to do the talking when it came time to share our decision. It was really hard saying no, especially when I was usually the one who wanted to let them go (Danielle and Eric, if you are reading this take note—I really was the fun parent!).

An important part of surviving the work/life balance dilemma is to have a good sense of humor and to be able to laugh at the situation. I've made certain mistakes my family won't let me live down. Instead of getting upset, I take them in stride. For example, one time I forgot to feed my kids dinner. As I've said, I'm not very good in the kitchen. It was a Saturday and my husband was on call. I was busy running errands with the kids, and yes, I just forgot. When Brad came home around 8 p.m., Eric mentioned he was hungry. Instead of getting angry, Brad cracked up, which made the kids laugh too. We toasted up some bagels and no one starved.

Then, there's the time I left my kids at religious school. Religious school was on Tuesdays and I did the evening pickup. That week, Monday was a holiday and, as a result, our favorite show, *Buffy the Vampire Slayer,* wasn't on. When Tuesday came, I was confused and thought it was Monday. I didn't really forget my children, I forgot what day it was! The kids survived and now they have the rest of their lives to tease me about it. As the saying goes, try not to sweat the small stuff.

My colleague Diana remarked it's essential to be realistic about what is possible when you work full time and that you aren't too hard on yourself. And don't be afraid to ask for help. "You can make it easier by finding a network of other parents who feel the same challenges and share resources and helpful ideas."

WRANGLING CHILDCARE

Assuming there are children involved, getting the right childcare is the most important aspect of balancing work and family. Each family's decision is different based on its unique circumstances, including its economic situation, the number of children, and the type of careers. Regardless of your choice, if you can be near family, that is preferable. When Brad and I ran into childcare issues or just needed a break from the kids, my parents often stepped in to help.

Brad and I opted for live-in childcare as soon as our first child was born because our schedules included long and unpredictable hours and business travel. Having someone live with you takes getting used to and we had our ups and downs, especially in the beginning. One advantage of this arrangement? When our kids were very young, they didn't need to get up early to go anywhere, so we kept them up late. Some people thought we were criminals for letting Danielle and Eric stay up until 10 or even 11 p.m. But since the kids slept in, they still got plenty of rest, and we got lots of time together. If I got home at six, we'd have four or five hours—plenty of time for playing, bath time, and reading.

Most people will tell you the hardest part of having children when you're a working parent is finding quality childcare. Brad and I were fortunate to have several people stay with us for five years or more, but there were certainly a few duds in there. Your life will be so much less stressful if you put the right time and effort into smart interviewing and especially those reference calls to other parents who employed the nanny, babysitter, or daycare provider previously.

Some working parents are concerned their children will love the babysitter more than them. I always thought that was a bit silly. The best thing that could happen is for your child to love their babysitter. It's wonderful to know your child is in such good hands. The presence of another loving adult in your child's life will never diminish the fact that you're the mother or father. You're going to be there for the long haul, the teenage heartbreaks, the college searches, and the wedding planning. No one will love your child like you do, and in turn, they will always love you uniquely as well.

1+1=11

Around the same time I fell in love with Miss Grasenflug, I also thought I wanted four sons. I planned to name them Kyle, Joel, Trevor, and Tracy. I guess I was an impressionable young child because there was a TV show called *Please Don't Eat the Daisies* that ran from 1965-1966, and surprise, the family had four sons with those very names!

For me, having children was never a question. My successful business career was a bit of a surprise, but it didn't preclude my desire for a family. Having one child was manageable. However, going from one to two was exponential and four was out of the question. Of course, I adore both my children and wouldn't do anything differently. I think it is important, though, to carefully consider how and when to extend your family.

GUILT COMPLEXES

Guilt is the cousin of regret and I've done a pretty good job keeping it at bay. For me, working was meaningful and I knew I would be a more engaged parent on my terms. But perhaps your main motivation for working is financial. Either reason is good enough justification. Being great at your job, providing for your family, and being a great parent aren't mutually exclusive!

One effective strategy is to compartmentalize. When my kids were younger and I was at the office, I was fully engaged. And honestly, unless there was a crisis at home, I was able to focus my attention on work. Conversely, when I was home, I was fully engaged with my kids and husband. If one of my kids crossed a big milestone, like taking their first steps, I said it didn't really count until I was there to witness it. Call me delusional if you want, but I chose not to let these sorts of things get me down.

I made a point to be present for most important events, such as the first day of school, the class play, or a key soccer match. I was fortunate my company and bosses over the years were agreeable to this and our company culture supports it. However, I was careful not to come across as entitled. I earned the right to leave for personal reasons because I regularly put in extra hours when needed.

I tried to be pragmatic too. I wish we could have had more family dinners together, but our schedules didn't work that way. My husband rarely made it home before 7:30 p.m., which was too late for the kids. So, we didn't have perfect family meals like you see on TV, where everyone sits around and shares details from their day. Family dinners might indeed be something you choose to prioritize, but for us, having the babysitter feed the kids earlier made the evenings smoother. It wasn't perfect, but it was "good enough."

Similarly, while it would have been nice to see my children in the morning, I discovered this was disruptive and often resulted in tears when it was time for me to leave. It was better for everyone if I spent quality time with my family in the evening instead. My routine involved getting into the office by 7:30 a.m. so I could leave around 5 p.m. This made for a long day, but luckily for me, I was power-napping long before Google put nap pods in its offices. Sometimes I'd get home, and before entering the house, would take a quick snooze in my car. Just 10 minutes gave me renewed vigor to take on two energetic kids.

QUALITY TIME IN TODAY'S CONNECTED WORLD

Today, it's admittedly harder to compartmentalize. After all, we have real-time access to a baby cam at home and/or daycare, and technology also connects us to our work 24/7. But we need to try as hard as we can to separate the personal and professional so we can be present in our present.

Widespread connectivity has an advantage, and that's increased flexibility. Parents can leave work early, have dinner with their families, and, after some quality time, catch up on work. They can take time off to attend school field day while remaining reachable by cell in case that important client happens to call.

Technology also makes it easier on families when someone has to travel. My husband and I are not great over the phone. We tend to be brusque with each other, and it isn't satisfying for either of us. When I went on my first trip to Asia for almost two weeks, I was very concerned. We decided to video chat, which was amazing. When my husband was able to see me, he was a different person than just on the phone. He was happy and silly, turning the screen upside down, making funny faces and laughing. Believe it or not, this went on for the whole trip. Just seeing each other for a few minutes a day closed the nearly 10,000 mile gap between us.

We didn't have iPads or Netflix in the '90s, so it was more challenging to keep the kids preoccupied. Don't get me wrong—our VCR served as a babysitter more than I'd care to admit. We watched *The Little Mermaid* until the tape practically disintegrated and we kept the local video store in business with how many times we rented *The Land Before Time*. People are quick to judge, and they shouldn't be until they've walked in your shoes. Let's be realistic—there are times when you need to get something done, so you stick your kid in front of the TV or take them out for fast food because you ran out of time to prepare a healthier option. Kids are pretty resilient and, as long as you aren't letting them put knives in the toaster, it's probably going to be fine. Just do the best you can and don't beat yourself up too much.

When you're a working parent, finding activities that allow for meaningful time together can be challenging. Reading is an especially good one and when my kids were pre-school age, I read to them almost every night. I love libraries and we went every Saturday. Each child picked six books a week. While it is easier to download books today, I still recommend the library. It's a fun and free outing, and you can use the money you save to get someone to do your laundry.

At a parenting seminar many years ago, the expert recommended giving each child a set amount of time every night (or as often as feasible) to choose whatever they want to do. This time is completely kid-directed. My only rule when employing this strategy? The activity couldn't involve watching TV. Sometimes my kids pooled their time and we all did something together. During kid time, we played board games, drew pictures, or, if their father wasn't home to disapprove, we vaulted Nerf balls around.

Parents had a terrific gem for moms and dads who have to occasionally work at home when the kids are around. Keep a hidden box filled with special toys that only comes out when you are on an important call or need to meet a work deadline. It works very well for kids (and dogs!) if you have the discipline to use the box only in emergencies.

One of my colleagues saved himself lots of time by buying his daughter a trunk load of gifts so when he came home from a business trip, he had something ready to go. The only catch? She found out about this years later and wasn't too happy he didn't take the time to find a gift from each city.

When it comes to work and family, it takes practice to get the right balance. I color code my calendar (pink for personal matters, yellow for external clients, blue for corporate meetings, and so on) and review it regularly to make sure I am spending time and energy in the right places—not necessarily every day, but over time.

Establishing boundaries that work for you is important too. For instance, my colleague Diana sets aside "phone free times." The first hour or two after she gets home at night, her phone is away so she can focus on being present with her family. That means no interruptions, whether work or personal. If it's really time-sensitive and critical, someone actually has to call Diana's home line!

Words of Wisdom

"Periodically ask yourself two questions. 1. Are you doing your job well? 2. Are you making a difference? The answer to both should be yes: that is the sweet spot of success."

—Lynda Firey-Oldroyd, senior director, Consumer Research, Starbucks.

MAKING TIME FOR HOBBIES AND GIVING

For me, having a full-time job and a family involved a trade-off. I didn't have much time for hobbies and charitable endeavors. Now that my children are older, I use my extra time to balance my work life with other meaningful activities. If you had told me years ago I would exercise for fun, I would have said you were crazy, but now I can't live without it. As I mentioned earlier, I've been inspired by a book targeted to my age group called *Younger Next Year*. When it comes to this topic, the gist of the book is: work out six days a week and don't eat crap.

Speaking of exercise, the key is to find something you like so it isn't just another chore. I love tennis and enjoy Pilates too. I run or go on the elliptical if I can watch TV at the same time. I'm a big fan of killing two birds with one stone. My son Eric is a runner who completed the New York City marathon this year. While I don't love running, I like to go for short runs with him because he has to do all the talking and I get to hear what is going on in his life!

I enjoy reading mystery and science fiction novels, but they are typically a vacation pastime. I was an early adopter of books on tape and now I subscribe to Audible. I can sync my Kindle book to the audio version, allowing me to catch up on my reading while running or driving in my car.

In terms of charitable work, Eric introduced me to the Resolution Project, and through him, I've gotten involved and joined their Advisory Board. The group's mission is to develop socially-responsible young leaders and empower them to make a positive impact today. It selects Resolution Fellows through Social Venture Challenges held around the world. Eric and I have attended several of these as judges. It's a win all around because I get to participate in an amazing program while spending time with my son.

For the past two years, I've also participated in a feed the needy Thanksgiving dinner at a local community center. They cleverly do it on the Sunday before Thanksgiving so it doesn't interfere with family time. I was a little nervous about what to expect, but luckily, I didn't have to cook. I've been responsible for serving and have found it to be a deeply rewarding experience.

EMPLOYERS INCREASE SHARE OF RESPONSIBILITY

In the last few years, many organizations have stepped up their efforts to retain top talent by promoting benefits that allow employees to better balance their personal and professional lives. Although the U.S. still lags behind much of the western world in terms of paid parental leave, Netflix made headlines with an announcement that it would offer employees a year of paid leave following the birth or adoption of a child. Google currently gives female employees 18 weeks of paid maternity leave, and Microsoft provides paid parental leave for 12 weeks to both genders.

If you aren't planning to have a child during your tenure, many companies will still look out for you! Consumer goods company

Colgate-Palmolive, for example, puts its vision of "healthy balance between work and personal responsibilities" into action with programs like tuition reimbursement, and health, legal, and financial counseling services.

For its part, news distribution firm Marketwired encourages employees to be active in their communities outside of work. It organizes volunteerism events throughout the year, and employees get one day off every quarter to make a difference at an organization close to their hearts.

Digital media startup OwnLocal thinks that fit employees are the most productive employees, so it outfits every hire with a Fitbit fitness tracker that tracks activity level and calorie intake. The company then sponsors an organization-wide competition to determine who has developed the healthiest habits.

And last, but not least, Home sharing giant Airbnb extends its mission of "travel often, travel globally, and travel together," to its employees. Every hire is given $2K per year (and the requisite vacation time) to fly anywhere in the world!

THE NAME GAME

Believe it or not, what you decide to call yourself definitely has an impact. When I got married in 1983, I decided to keep my maiden name, Schoenbart, at work. Since I was in sales at the time, I felt my name had equity. I also decided to change my legal name to my husband's name, because I didn't like the idea of having a different last name than my someday children. It was a little confusing at the dry cleaners and restaurants if I couldn't remember which name I used, but overall, I managed. At that time, you could travel on airplanes and book hotels under any name you wanted. However, after 9/11, things changed and now you're required to travel under your legal name.

Anyone who makes travel plans for me now knows to book them under Sporkin. Frankly, it is a bit of a mess—my business card is Schoenbart, my paycheck is Sporkin. It's a good thing they both start with an "S" because I changed my signature to Karyn S, so it works for both mes. If I had it to do over, I think I would either stick with Schoenbart legally or switch to Sporkin for everything. At 26, my name probably didn't have as much equity as I thought it did.

For married women and increasingly for married men, this is a personal decision and there isn't a right or wrong answer. I do recommend investigating all your options and thinking through the potential unintended consequences for the long-term.

TIME MANAGEMENT HACKS

Beyond outsourcing as much as you can, it helps to be steadfast in your time management. Multi-tasking is your friend. Here are a few tips that have worked for me:

- If you have to do a chore you're not crazy about, involve one of your kids and try to make it a game.
- I designed an Excel spreadsheet based on the aisles of my local supermarket and hung it on the refrigerator. Whenever we were out of something, any family member could mark it on the sheet. Each week, I'd simply go up and down the aisles and pick up what we needed.
- I have a master packing checklist for traveling. I often almost forget something like a hair clip or a phone charger, so the list is my savior.
- I used to suffer from FOMO (fear of missing out). Now I prefer GTSE (going to sleep early). It's okay to skip things

and not help everyone all the time. Your real friends will understand. Weed the others from your life.

- If you feel out of balance, find a sliver of time for yourself. Even if it is just a half hour a day to do something that makes you happy or helps you relax, it's worth it. My favorite is a massage, but if I can't get there, a bubble bath will do.
- Share a Google calendar with your spouse. My colleague Diana claimed this is the only way she and her husband know who has what when, when schools are closed, if they need to juggle pick up/drop off schedules, or if they need to call in reinforcements!
- Speaking of calendars, I've blocked my calendar after 4:30 p.m. every day. I may have to schedule something after 4:30 p.m., but this makes me think twice before doing so.
- Take the vacation you've earned and recharge! As Diana said: "You can't take care of anyone else if you are not taking care of yourself."

In the end, I don't think my family has suffered as a result of my career. Of course, I made my share of mistakes, but all parents do, and I'm sure even my childhood idol Mary Poppins made some. I like to think my kids thrived because my husband and I were good role models. They have great careers of their own and are in healthy relationships with people we adore. We are all close and enjoy spending time together. Our daughter and son have seen firsthand you can be passionate about your career while still being devoted to your family. I'm not sure what having it all really means, but this is good enough for me!

Words of Wisdom

"Recognize that it's hard for everyone at times. Just go for it, and when something feels right, dig in more and enjoy the journey!"

—Howard Applebaum, president, Nielsen Entertainment.

SURVEY SAYS: PROGRESS ON WORK AND LIFE BALANCE

Work/life balance gets a bad rap. Especially in the U.S. popular wisdom indicates having both a healthy and successful personal AND professional life is virtually impossible. However, one study by Robert Half Management Resources paints a much more optimistic picture. The staffing agency surveyed over 2,000 chief financial officers from companies in more than 20 of the largest U.S. metropolitan areas and 1,000 U.S. workers employed in office environments. More than three-quarters of workers described their work/life balance as very good and exactly where they want it to be, or good and close to where they want it to be.

Surprisingly, work/life balance looked even better from the perspective of senior executives: 82 percent of company leaders rated their work/life balance as good or very good. And only two percent of workers and three percent of executives said their balance is poor or they don't have any balance at all. Forty-five percent of all Robert Half's respondents said their work/life balance has gotten better in the past three years, while only 14 percent said it has gotten worse.

Given the meteoric rise of dual-income families (according to Pew Research, 46 percent of two-parent households include both a mom and dad who work full time), how exactly are working moms and dads juggling things in order to achieve this level of personal and professional harmony? CivicScience CEO John Dick offered a clue in his recent article for the *Huffington Post*. In his discussion of the "domesticated dad," Dick indicated men are pitching in far more at home than they used to, which contributes to better balance for traditionally frazzled working women. In a recent CivicScience survey, 33 percent of working dads said they do most of the cooking in their households, 42 percent do most of the grocery shopping, and 14 percent make ALL the household and children's purchases.

These developments offer hope to anyone who hopes to devote enough attention to both personal and professional endeavors and stay sane in the process!

CHAPTER SUMMARY

- To quote Oprah Winfrey: "You can have it all, but you can't have it all at once." You need to decide what having it all means for you. Even if you are lucky enough to simultaneously manage a successful career and a family, there inevitably will be some sacrifices required along the way.
- Outsource what you can so you can spend time doing things you love with the people you love. When faced with a bevy of time-consuming chores, paying for occasional assistance really will improve the quality of your life!
- Being great at your job, providing for your family, and being a great parent aren't mutually exclusive. Manage both effectively by compartmentalizing. When you're at work, be fully engaged there—and vice versa. Be present in your present.
- There are times when you just need to get something done and you stick your kid in front of the TV. Kids are pretty resilient and it's probably going to be fine. Just do the best you can and don't beat yourself up too much.
- Widespread connectivity also has an advantage, and that's increased flexibility. But establishing your own boundaries is critical, as is figuring out what the right balance looks like for you.
- An important part of surviving the work/life balance dilemma is to have a good sense of humor and to be able to

laugh at the situation. Try not to sweat the small stuff and be realistic about what is possible given your work situation.

Words of Wisdom

"Create a purpose out of life. Do what you love and follow your heart."

—Ali Charri, senior vice president, Strategy and Insights, Darden Restaurants.

APPENDIX:

IT TAKES A VILLAGE

I WOULDN'T BE ABLE to do my job successfully without the insights of my colleagues at the NPD Group. I hope their collective words of wisdom help you as much as they've helped me.

"My dad always reinforced three rules in business. Listen more than you talk, don't be afraid to ask questions, and don't be afraid to say 'I don't know.' I'd encourage everyone to practice these habits to improve their personal effectiveness and impact."

—Jeremy Allen, group president, Product Management and Development, NPD Group.

"As you enter the business world, transform into a sponge. Soak in everything around you. Align yourself with the company's key objectives and those of your supervisor. Focus on how you can contribute to the organization's success and your success will follow."

—Dennis Brown, group operating officer, NPD Group.

"Failing is part of success. Learn from your mistakes as they can have

more impact on your future success than some of the big wins in life."

—Tim Bush, group president, NPD Group.

"Go deep. Whatever task is set before you, dive into it fully. Understand its context, why it is being done, how it interacts with other tasks, and how it could be done more efficiently. Go wide. Aim to graduate yourself every 18 months in the early stages of your working life. By building experiences in operational, analytical, creative, and human interaction tasks, you'll push your ceiling ever higher."

—Steve Coffey, chief innovation officer, NPD Group.

"Work very hard and don't make the same mistake twice."

—Virginia Grande, global head, Human Resources, NPD Group.

"The harder you work, the luckier you will be."

—Tom Lynch, CFO, NPD Group.

"Understand your environment and bring innovation to clients. Be paranoid about competition, invest in people and relationships, and keep a close eye on costs and expenses as if it was your own company."

—Michel Maury, group president, Europe and Asia, NPD Group.

"Be inquisitive. Take chances. Believe in the courage of your convictions. Have fun. And remember, everyone makes mistakes – it's what you do with them that's important. Recognize them, learn from them, and move on."

—Diane Nicholson, group president,
Beauty, Fashion, and Sports, NPD Group.

"Always be prepared! Read materials in advance of any meeting and

formulate a point of view, but also be prepared to learn from others' perspectives. When you start out, the amount of information coming at you can be overwhelming, but the better you listen, the quicker you learn."

—Vicki Niems, senior vice president, NPD Group.

"Take initiative and be persistent, but be thoughtful about it."

—Susan Pechman, chief marketing officer, NPD Group.

"Stay positive always, look for the good in everyone, take all advice, and assume that your more senior colleagues want you to succeed: they've found their way and will help you find yours."

—George Terhanian, group president and chief research and analytics officer, NPD Group.

"Fall in love with your company's business model first. Is the company growing? How easy is the business model to duplicate? Does the ethical code match yours? Then, fall in love with the people at the company. This goes for the people you will work for and work with. Fall in love with the compensation last."

—Don Unser, group president, Retail, Financial Services, and Public Sector, NPD Group.

ACKNOWLEDGEMENTS

WHILE MY DAUGHTER was the inspiration for this book, nothing would be possible if it weren't for my wonderful parents, Anita and Zelman Schoenbart. My father was my first business hero and my mother instilled in me a love for people and a knack for remembering names. They always encouraged my brother Steve and me, and through their unconditional love and support they showed us that anything is possible.

I was so lucky to find Alexandra Levit, with whom I collaborated on Mom.B.A. Alexandra has authored several business books, including the international bestseller, *They Don't Teach Corporate in College*. She generously shared her experience and advice with me and through the intimate experience of writing this book, we've become good friends.

My husband Brad put up with me holed away on too many weekends and vacations trying to write this "in my spare time" while still running a multi-million dollar corporation. He provided a great sounding board, even when he'd rather we be doing something else. His never-ending support for me and all I want to do is one of the greatest gifts a spouse can give. My children, Danielle and Eric, were gracious enough to let me use them in this book, and even allowed me to tell some embarrassing stories about them. They were my unofficial proofreaders, ensuring that the final product didn't have any misplaced commas or too many exclamation points!

One of the most joyous parts of my job is that I get to learn new things every day. Deep thanks to all of my business associates who took the time to provide their "words of wisdom" and also my colleagues at NPD who lent their support and business advice, including Jeremy, Dennis, Tim, Steve, Virginia, Tom, Michel, Diane, Vicki, Susan, George, Heather, Kelly, Danielle, and Donna. And special thanks to Tod Johnson for his support over so many years of working together. You're the best of the best!

Finally, since life is more than just work, I am grateful for the friends who keep me grounded and who shared stories of their own journeys: Carrie and Randi, who are more like family than friends: Lisa and Rob, who have been my personal fan club: Morgan, who believed I could do this book before I did: and my tennis buddies, Bonnie, Denise, Ellen, Janie, Maggi and Winkie.

BIBLIOGRAPHY

CHAPTER ONE SOURCES

Etcoff, N. L., Stock, S., Haley, L. E., Vickery, S. A., & House, D. M. (2011). Cosmetics as a Feature of the Extended Human Phenotype: Modulation of the Perception of Biologically Important Facial Signals. *PLOS*, doi: 10.1371/journal.pone.0025656.

Friedman, Ann. 2015. *Can We Just, Like, Get Over the Way Women Talk?* New York Magazine. http://nymag.com/thecut/2015/07/can-we-just-like-get-over-the-way-women-talk.html

Guadagno, R. E., & Cialdini, R. B. (2007). Gender differences in impression management in organizations: A qualitative review. *Sex Roles,* 56, 483–494. doi: 10.1007/s11199-007-9187-3.

Haskamp, Jennie. 2017. 15 *Words You Need to Eliminate from Your Vocabulary to Sound Smarter*. The Muse. Retrieved 2017, from https://www.themuse.com/advice/15-words-you-need-to-eliminate-from-your-vocabulary-to-sound-smarter

McAleer, P., Todorov, A., & Belin, P. (2014). How Do You Say 'Hello'? Personality Impressions from Brief Novel Voices. *PLOS*, doi: 10.1371/journal.pone.0090779.

Naumann, L. P., Vazire, S., Rentfrow, P. J., & Gosling, S. D. (2009). Personality judgments based on physical appearance. *Personality and Social Psychology Bulletin,* 35, 1661–1671. doi: 10.1177/0146167209346309.

Senge, Peter. T*he Fifth Discipline: The Art & Practice of the Learning Organization*. New York, NY: Doubleday, 2006.

CHAPTER TWO SOURCES

Johnson, Susan. 2015. *Networking is Over. Welcome Sweatworking?* Fast Company. https://www.fastcompany.com/3047240/how-to-be-a-success-at-everything/networking-is-over-welcome-sweatworking

McKeown, Greg. 2015. *99% of Networking is a Waste of Time.* Harvard Business Review. https://hbr.org/2015/01/99-of-networking-is-a-waste-of-time

The Meetology Group. 2013. *The Meetology Laboratory 2012 Behavioural Research Results.* Meetology.com. http://meetology.com

Misner, Ivan. 2011. *Online Networks Lag Behind Other Networking Efforts*. IvanMisner.com. http://ivanmisner.com/onlinenetworkslag/

Morrow, Monika. 2013. *Networking, Not Internet Cruising, Still Lands Most Jobs for Those in Career Transition.* Right Management. http://www.right.com/wps/wcm/connect/right-us-en/home/thoughtwire/categories/talent-work/networking-not-internet-cruising-still-lands-most-jobs-for-those-in-career-transition

Keller, Ed & Fay, Brad. *The Face-to-Face Book: Why Real Relationships Rule in a Digital Marketplace.* New York, NY: Free Press, 2012.

Small, Gary. *iBrain: Surviving the Technological Alteration of the Modern Mind.* New York, NY: HarperCollins, 2009.

CHAPTER THREE SOURCES

Brooks, Chad. 2013. *Workers in the Dark About What Bosses Want.* Business News Daily.
http://www.businessnewsdaily.com/4015-workers-unclear-about-job-expectations.html

Duppins, Melanie. 2015. *6 Ways to Make Your Boss Love You.* WorkItDaily (formerly CareerRealism). https://www.workitdaily.com/make-boss-love-you-ways/

Jacobs, AJ. 2015. *5 Terrible Types of Bosses from History.* Mental Floss. http://mentalfloss.com/article/68503/5-terrible-types-bosses-history

Matta, F. K., Scott, B., Colquitt, J., Koopman, J., & Passantino, L. (2016). Is Consistently Unfair Better than Sporadically Fair? An Investigation of Justice Variability and Stress. *Academy of Management Journal*, 59.6, doi:10.5465/amj.2014.0455.

Melen, Thomas. 2011. *Job ads reflect society and working life.* University of Gothenburg. http://hum.gu.se/english/current/news/Nyhet_detalj/job-ads-reflect-society-and-working-life.cid1025981

Schawbel, Dan. 2013. *7 Things Managers Look for When Promoting.* The Fast Track. http://www.quickbase.com/blog/7-things-managers-look-for-when-promoting

CHAPTER FOUR SOURCES

Bensen, Tracy. 2016. *Motivating Millennials Takes More than Flexible Work Policies.* Harvard Business Review. https://hbr.

org/2016/02/motivating-millennials-takes-more-than-flexible-work-policies

Cohan, Peter. 2013. *Adobe's Stock Up 68% Since It Dumped Stack Ranking, Will Microsoft's Follow?* Forbes. http://www.forbes.com/sites/petercohan/2013/11/29/adobes-stock-up-68-since-it-dumped-stack-ranking-will-microsofts-follow/#44e369b13690

Gajendran, R., Somaya, D. 2016. *Employees Leave Good Bosses Nearly as Often as Bad Ones.* Harvard Business Review. https://hbr.org/2016/03/employees-leave-good-bosses-nearly-as-often-as-bad-ones

Gallup. 2014. *State of the American Manager: Analytics and Advice for Leaders.* Gallup.com.
http://www.gallup.com/services/182138/state-american-manager.aspx

Nelson, Bob. *Secrets of Successful Employee Recognition.* Quality Digest. Accessed 2017, from http://www.qualitydigest.com/aug/nelson.html

Son, Sabrina. 2015. *The Real Reason Why Millennials Crave Feedback in the Workplace.* TINYpulse.com. https://www.tinypulse.com/blog/sk-the-real-reason-why-millennials-in-the-workplace-crave-feedback-in-the-workplace

TINYpulse. 2012. *The Effects of Employee Recognition and Appreciation.* TINYpulse.com.
https://www.tinypulse.com/resources/the-effects-of-employee-recognition-and-appreciation

CHAPTER FIVE SOURCES

The Empowerment Partnership. *What is NLP?* NLP.com. Accessed 2017, from http://www.nlp.com/

Glassdoor. 2015. *More Than Sixty Percent Of U.S. Workers Admit To Workplace Mistakes Due To Tiredness.* PRNewswire.com. http://www.prnewswire.com/news-releases/more-than-sixty-percent-of-us-workers-admit-to-workplace-mistakes-due-to-tiredness-300019693.html

Pearson, Christine and Porath, Christine. 2013. *The Price of Incivility.* Harvard Business Review. https://hbr.org/2013/01/the-price-of-incivility

Porath, Christine. 2015. *No Time to Be Nice at Work.* The New York Times. https://www.nytimes.com/2015/06/21/opinion/sunday/is-your-boss-mean.html?_r=0

CHAPTER SIX SOURCES

Babcock, Linda, and Laschever, Sara. *Women Don't Ask: Negotiation and the Gender Divide.* Princeton, NJ: Princeton University Press, 2009.

Babcock, Linda, and Laschever, Sara. *Ask For It: How Women Can Use Negotiation to Get What They Really Want.* New York, NY: Bantam, 2008.

Clay, Robert. *Why 8% of sales people get 80% of the sales.* MarketingDonut.co.uk. Accessed 2017, from http://www.marketingdonut.co.uk/sales/sales-techniques-and-negotiations/why-8-of-sales-people-get-80-of-the-sales

Cubed, Jeffa. *The Boilermaker Story—Or Knowing Where to Tap.* JeffaCubed.com. Accessed 2017, from http://jeffacubed.com/the-boilermaker-story-or-knowing-where-to-tap/

Gallwey, W. Timothy. *The Inner Game of Tennis: The Classic Guide to the Mental Side of Peak Performance*. New York, NY: Random House, 2010.

Payscale, Inc. 2015. *PayScale Announces 2015 Salary Negotiation Guide.* Payscale.com. http://www.payscale.com/about/press-releases/payscale-announces-2015-salary-negotiation-guide

Pemberton, Steve. "Age-Activated Attention Deficit Disorder." Online video clip. YouTube.com, 2008. Accessed 2017, from https://www.youtube.com/watch?v=6oHBG3ABUJU&t=93s

CHAPTER SEVEN SOURCES

Berger, Guy. 2016. *Most Popular Cities and Jobs for Americans Working Abroad.* LinkedIn.com. https://blog.linkedin.com/2016/07/28/Most-Popular-Cities-and-Jobs-for-Americans-Working-Abroad

InterNations. What is an Expat Anyway? InterNations.org. Accessed 2017, from https://www.internations.org/magazine/what-s-an-expat-anyway-15272

Mercer. 2015. *Global Employee Mobility—Increased Diversification Across Types of International Assignments Used.* Mercer.com. https://www.mercer.com/newsroom/global-employee-mobility-increased-diversification-across-types-of-international-assignments-used.html

Mercer. 2015. *Worldwide Survey of International Assignment Policies and Practices.* iMercer.com. https://www.imercer.com/products/WorldwideIAPP.aspx

Platt, Polly. *French or Foe: Getting the Most Out of Visiting, Living and Working in France.* Skokie, IL: Distribooks, 2003.

PricewaterhouseCoopers. 2012. *Talent Mobility: 2020 and Beyond.* PWC.com.
https://www.pwc.com/gx/en/managing-tomorrows-people/future-of-work/pdf/pwc-talent-mobility-2020.pdf

RW3/Culture Wizard. 2016. *Trends in Global Virtual Teams.* CultureWizard.com. http://cdn.culturewizard.com/PDF/Trends_in_VT_Report_4-17-2016.pdf

Vance, C. M., McNulty, Y., Paik, Y., & D'Mello, J. (2016). The Expat-preneur: conceptualizing a growing international career phenomenon. *Journal of Global Mobility*, 4.2, 204-224, doi:10.1108/JGM-11-2015-0055.

CHAPTER EIGHT SOURCES

Abbott, Marty and Fisher, Michael. *The Art of Scalability: Scalable Web Architecture, Processes, and Organizations for the Modern Enterprise.* Boston, MA: Addison-Wesley Professional, 2015.

Bradt, George. 2016. *Two-Way Time Management For Senior Executives.* Forbes. http://www.forbes.com/sites/georgebradt/2016/08/17/two-way-time-management-for-senior-executives/#6c7224a758e7

Bryant, Adam. 2016. *Be Sure to Tell the Boss What's Wrong.* The New York Times. https://www.nytimes.com/2016/08/21/business/bracken-darrell-of-logitech-be-sure-to-tell-the-boss-whats-wrong.html

Leadership. *Wikipedia, The Free Encyclopedia.* Retrieved 2017 from, https://en.wikipedia.org/w/index.php?title=Leadership&oldid=762232400

Levit, Alexandra. 2016. *Race to the Top: Traits That Propel and Derail Senior Leaders.* The Fast Track. http://www.quickbase.

com/blog/race-to-the-top-traits-that-propel-and-derail-senior-leaders

Quote Investigator. 2015. *When Two Men in Business Always Agree, One of Them Is Unnecessary.* QuoteInvestigator.com. http://quoteinvestigator.com/2015/04/04/agree/

Rizkalla, Emad. 2016. *Why Corporate Culture Eats Strategy for Breakfast.* Huffington Post. http://www.huffingtonpost.com/emad-rizkalla/why-corporate-culture-eat_b_10573092.html

Sanborn, Mark. *You Don't Need a Title to Be a Leader: How Anyone, Anywhere, Can Make a Positive Difference.* New York, NY: Crown Business, 2006.

Sheridan, Bill. 2016. *Doing Nothing Will Kill You.* Business Learning Institute. http://blionline.org/2016/11/nothing-will-kill/

CHAPTER NINE SOURCES

Berger, Guy. 2016. *How to Become an Executive.* LinkedIn.com. https://www.linkedin.com/pulse/how-become-executive-guy-berger-ph-d-?published=t

Byrne, John. 2015. *Should You Get an MBA? Is the Degree Worth It?* LinkedIn.com. https://www.linkedin.com/pulse/should-you-get-mba-degree-worth-john-a-byrne

Clance, P.R. & Imes, S. (1978). The impostor phenomenon in high achieving women: Dynamics and therapeutic intervention. *Psychotherapy: Theory, Research and Practice,* 15, 241–247. doi: 10.1037/h0086006.

Pausch, Randy. *The Last Lecture.* New York, NY: Hyperion, 2008.

Randstad USA. 2014. *Sponsors Vs. Mentors: What's the Difference?*

Randstad USA Blogs. http://blogs.randstadusa.com/women-poweringbusiness/sponsors-vs-mentors-whats-the-difference/
Reinhold, Barbara. *Lateral Moves: When Do They Work?* Monster.com. Accessed 2017, from https://www.monster.com/career-advice/article/lateral-moves-when-do-they-work

CHAPTER TEN SOURCES

Adamczyk, Alicia. 2015. *These Are the Companies With the Best Parental Leave Policies.* Time. http://time.com/money/4098469/paid-parental-leave-google-amazon-apple-facebook/
Aristotle. 350 B.C.E. *Nicomachean Ethics and Politics.*
Dick, John. 2016. *Women Are Getting a Terrible Deal.* The Huffington Post. http://www.huffingtonpost.com/john-dick/women-are-getting-a-terri_b_11434842.html
Pew Research Center. 2015. *Raising Kids and Running a Household: How Working Parents Share the Load. PewSocialTrends.org.* http://www.pewsocialtrends.org/2015/11/04/raising-kids-and-running-a-household-how-working-parents-share-the-load/
Robert Half Management Resources. 2015. *More Than Three In Four Professionals Striking Work-Life Balance.* Robert Half Media Room. http://rhmr.mediaroom.com/work-life-balance-CFOs?_ga=1.89186779.1167658686.1485832347
Woodruff, Lisa. 2015. *10 Ways to Outsource Your Household Tasks.* Organize 365. https://organize365.com/10-ways-to-outsource-your-household-tasks/